CAROL MARTIN-SPERRY, an
and psychosexual therapist, l
couples and individuals for r
She trained with Relate and ....age
Guidance, where she was on the Board of Trustees
and founded the Counsellors Association. She manages a bilingual private practice in London and is
the author of *Couples and Sex: An Introduction to
Relationship Dynamics and Psychosexual Concepts*,
published by Radcliffe Publishing, and an online
book, *Good Sex, Bad Sex, No Sex*, which forms the
basis of a course she runs at the Skyros Centre. Carol
was awarded a Fellowship at the British Association
for Counselling and Psychotherapy in 2009, and
works as a broadcaster, writer and consultant on
counselling and therapeutic issues. She has represented the British Association for Counselling and
Psychotherapy as a media spokesperson since 1997.
She was named in the *Evening Standard* list of top
twenty therapists and profiled in the *Guardian*. For
more information, visit www.shrinkrap.co.uk

SEXUAL HEALING

Stories and insights from
the therapist's couch

Carol Martin-Sperry

Constable & Robinson Ltd
55–56 Russell Square
London WC1B 4HP
www.constablerobinson.com

First published in the UK by How to Books,
an imprint of Constable & Robinson, 2014

A copy of the British Library Cataloguing in Publication Data
is available from the British Library

ISBN: 978-1-84528-551-7 (paperback)
ISBN: 978-1-84528-565-4 (ebook)

1 3 5 7 9 10 8 6 4 2

Printed and bound in the EU

'Be a good animal, true to your instincts'
D.H. Lawrence

For my clients, who had the courage to share
their most intimate difficulties with me

Contents

Preface

This book looks at sexual issues in an informative, thoughtful and sometimes provocative way. It attempts to address the many questions that arise from our sexuality with a practical approach and psychological insight, illustrated by fascinating true stories. Names and details have been changed to protect anonymity.

Foreword

What I've always liked about Carol Martin Sperry's work is that I usually agree with what she says! *Sexual Healing* is no exception. We appear to be on the same page when it comes to attitudes to psychotherapy, sexuality and the importance of speaking up.

From the outset I admire her use of narrative. All the great therapies in the world are about the art of story-telling. That's how we learn. That's how we make art. That's how we frame relationships. By telling and repeating our stories. This is a really good book of tales about sex always with a purpose and a point.

Since therapists are not allowed to break clients' confidences, I also note that the stories in this book are rather more complicated to construct than you may realise. They are sufficiently doctored to remove identities but cleverly rearranged to provide the necessary insights. That's a rare skill. Carol is clearly both writer and therapist.

Carol manages to speak directly (as I am sure she does in the consulting room) without jargon while deploying the occasional pithy Anglo-Saxonism. At the same time, she has a grasp of theory which shames those who promote a kind of witless psychology where people represent cognitive robots or behavioural automata or uninterpretable brain maps. The inescapable fact which Carol so cleverly demonstrates is that we all come with emotional baggage from families which, generally-speaking, mistrained and misfitted us for easy relationships. It's why we experience sexual problems. There is almost NO sex therapy that simply consists in telling people they are using the wrong position or aperture. Sex therapy is really that branch of psychology focusing on human physical contact.

On the one hand there's sex – something god or Darwin-given, which is bigger than any of us and through which nature induces us to procreate almost regardless of cost. On the other hand, there's that baggage train of feelings. What gets in the way of the evolution of great sex is what our parents and life did to us before we were permitted to mature.

Question: why is this client's sexuality as it is? Answer: possibly because he was born to a depressed mum and controlling dad and then displaced by a golden sister. His survival strategy therefore consists in equal parts of depression, repression and narcissism. His sexual equipment works fine – in the privacy of his own trousers. But put him among desirable strangers and he may well suffer bouts of self-doubt, occasional erectile disorder, elements of commitment-phobia and episodes of bad temper.

Or perhaps he won't. What Carol demonstrates is the endless variety of puzzles that therapy helps us solve. As

I am fond of saying, therapy is hard work for all concerned, not least the therapist.

But her underlying message remains clear. Though most of us want and enjoy sex, to make it work throughout life (or until arthritis prevails) we need to understand our own biology and psychology. For instance, is your confidence great or small – often decided at birth as a by-product of your metabolism? Or is your sex drive higher or lower than the average on a bell-shaped curve? (A tiny minority of individuals want sex all day; an equally tiny group want sex rarely; while most of us fall in the middle). In terms of personality, are you a pleaser or a taker; a goody two shoes or a black sheep?

In effect, what roles do you adopt to get your way in the world – because it'll be the same in bed and you'll produce outcomes that are both similar and familiar. Partnerships are difficult precisely because there is this conflict between differing traditions of family attitude. Sometimes we need expert help from guides like Carol to discover our more freely chosen selves.

Phillip Hodson is a psychotherapist,
sex therapist, author and broadcaster associated
with the UK Council for Psychotherapy.
www.psychotherapy.org.uk
www.philliphodson.co.uk

Introduction:
Sex, Love and Therapy

As a psychotherapist working with couples I knew that sex was a vital element in every relationship, present even by its absence. Sex and sexuality affect each and every one of us, from childhood to old age. I have always been interested in the 'why' of sex, in its meaning and how it can be a power for bad as well as good.

Freud told us that our sexuality is at the heart of everything we are, whether or not we are aware of it, whether expressed or suppressed, and Darwin put the need to breed at the centre of being. Sex is where we come from and our sexuality is a major part of who we are. As Bill Shankly could have said, 'Sex is not just a matter of life and death, it's much more than that'.

The social and cultural evolution of our sexuality has moved much faster than our evolutionary physical development. We are in danger of becoming out of touch with our primitive drives and instincts. Add to this the continuing confusion about gender roles, the cult of the individual, unrealistic expectations, an increasing desire for instant gratification and the accompanying low tolerance of ambivalence and frustration and it's no wonder long-term committed relationships are becoming increasingly hard to sustain in a social environment of rapid change. Sex can become problematic. The conflict between our evolutionary drives and our changing societal and cultural roles is at the very heart of my stories.

Sex is one of the greatest pleasures in life. It's free and can easily take less than an hour. Every single one of us is a sexual being, whether or not we are having sex. With such a natural activity, surely it should be quite straightforward once you've got the hang of it? Yet many of us are having infrequent or unsatisfactory sex, or we are not having sex at all. What has gone wrong? Why is it so complicated, and what can we do to put it right?

We live in a society that emphasises sexuality, sex appeal and sexual gratification. All kinds of pornography are available on the Internet to satisfy our wildest fantasies. The media bombard us round the clock with endless images and messages. Too much information just adds to the confusion and gives us unrealistically high expectations. Often we feel let down and disappointed, or even incompetent and inadequate. What if we don't measure up?

'Was that it?'
'Was I good enough?'
'Am I getting enough?'
'Why am I not getting any?'

We come from a long cultural, religious and social history that has left behind a heritage of guilt and fear, shame and anxiety. And now there are gender role issues too.

> 'I want a man who is caring and nurturing, not some old-fashioned caveman. I want him to share things equally with me. But he's got to be sexy'

> 'My girlfriend is an independent career woman. She is strong and powerful. I find that a turn-on'

> 'I like my man to work hard and bring in the money so that I can look after the kids at home. It's old-fashioned, but it works for us. In the bedroom he makes the moves'

While New Man and Post-Feminist Woman try to work out a more equal sexual relationship, Macho Man and Trad Woman are alive and well, if sometimes unsure about how to conduct their love lives. We all seem to be under pressure to perform. Sometimes it's easier to cop out, but what are we missing?

What exactly is good sex? Different people give different answers.

> 'It's such a rush, so exciting; it makes me hot and breathless. There is nothing in the world that can make me feel so good!'

> 'It makes me feel connected, it's intimate, it's bonding'

'I only have to look at her and I get that adrenal surge in my guts'

One of the most wonderful things about sex is how broad an experience it can be, from the merest touch to passionate lovemaking, and everything in between.

Sex can be thrilling and lustful, the ultimate in pleasure. Or it can be a shared moment of tenderness and intimacy. It can be playful and fun, it can be anonymous and dangerous, it can be simple and straightforward, or a sophisticated and complex game. You may have soulmate sex or stranger sex and it can still be good. Good sex is all of this and more.

When sex is added to romantic love it can transcend everything, leading to intoxicating feelings of ecstasy and bliss. It can be so intense and overwhelming that it becomes all-consuming, obsessive even. Think of Romeo and Juliet, Cathy and Heathcliff, Anna Karenina, Madame Bovary . . . The literary list is endless and reflects some eternal truths about the powerful nature of love and sex. As for pop songs, love and sex are what most of them are about.

Falling in love is such a powerful event because it puts us back in that state of newborn bliss. Our first experience of love is in the intense attachment to the mother who (ideally) gives total care and attention, unconditional love and responds to all our needs. It is through this exclusive bond that the baby develops basic trust and security and the ability to be close and intimate in later life. Baby and mother are merged in blissful union. But with love come separation, anxiety and the fear of loss and abandonment; it doesn't come without risk.

Falling in love brings the hope of reliving a union as perfect as the mother/baby relationship and the desire to be merged and never be alone. When lovers look into each other's eyes they seek the reflected loving gaze of their mothers' eyes, a world of safety and intimacy. But they are also connected to the fear of loss and the possibility of disappointment, frustration and anger.

The closer we are to our partners, the closer we are to our inner selves. Love can put us in touch with our inner strengths but it can also reveal the hidden feelings that have been repressed because they are unacceptable, shameful or too painful. We fall in love hoping to be freed from the problems caused by painful experiences. A profound relationship with the right partner provides a place of safety, an emotional container and a chance to work through past difficulties.

The intense and passionate honeymoon sex phase can last for months, even years. But eventually it needs to transform from a passionate and romantic ideal into something more realistic. Some people find it very difficult to move from 'in love' to 'loving'. They are hooked on the excitement and the buzz of hot sex. The desire to keep feeling the thrill of the new often leads to serial relationships, flings and affairs.

Sex is different at different ages and stages. Things can go wrong for a variety of reasons. Sometimes there are physical problems such as erectile difficulties or painful sex. Sometimes our sex lives are affected by particular events in our lives such as illness, work problems or family issues. Sometimes we simply get bored or lazy, or even too busy for sex. The same old routine is just too dull, we can't be bothered and then we get out of the habit. Often we neglect to talk to each other, we take each other for granted; we are at risk of an affair. Monogamy can be hard work, but infidelity hurts.

Anger and anxiety are the enemies of good sex, as are guilt and shame. Often they can set up a self-perpetuating vicious circle of fear of failure. Many sexual difficulties that express themselves physically in the body are of psychological origin, confirming that the brain is our most important sexual organ. We are conditioned by our experiences and memories.

There may be deeper problems with drink and drugs, addiction or a history of abuse. Sex can be exploitative and manipulative; it can be used as a bargaining chip, a way of controlling one's partner. But so too can withholding sex – it's a powerful tool. Desire is a mystery. It comes and it goes from 'I really want you' to 'I just don't fancy you any more'. It's as much psychological as physical, fed by thoughts, feelings and fantasies as well as sensations. So many factors can affect desire that it's hard to identify them all. Perhaps we expect too much of our partners and ourselves?

Bad sex includes behaviour driven by compulsion and the need for power and control. It can be violent and debasing, sordid and shameful, bizarre and risky. Chosen objects (i.e. fetishistic and sexualised objects) and situations that are compulsively repeated take on a particular sexual meaning. Hatred may be eroticised through sado-masochistic practices. When there is a lack of mutual consent and imposed secrecy, when boundaries are broken, sex becomes abuse.

Bad sex usually comes with a history of early emotional deprivation and frustration, a desperate and narcissistic need for satisfaction or even punishment, expressed in the acting out of taboo desires and fantasies. 'Sad' sex is another form of bad sex, when sex becomes dutiful and dull, or is affected by repression, inhibition or ignorance. So is anonymous sex, often illicit, with no degree of intimacy but some degree of thrill, bad sex? Men – and it is almost always men – who frequent prostitutes, massage parlours, lap-dancing clubs, or who indulge in kerb crawling, voyeurism or exhibitionism, are usually unable to sustain a lasting and profound monogamous sexual relationship. The repetition of bad sex in situations they can control, either with force or by payment, brings temporary respite to their frustrated desires.

With the advent of Internet porn, swap clubs and secret orgies, sexual behaviour is breaching new frontiers in the search for increasing novelty and stimulation. Anything is permitted. Children are becoming sexualised at an even earlier age. Sex is marketed as an activity where instant gratification is encouraged and expected.

The emotional and psychological fallout of bad sex is considerable, not just for the victim but also for the instigator. As a client group they both need sensitive work with an experienced and confident therapist, who will maintain firm boundaries.

Sex will always have the power to surprise us. It can bring profound joy, it can bring new life, but it can also destroy and even kill us. It can be dangerous, which in turn makes it even more exciting. Sex is how and what you want it to be at the time, a unique experience shared with another person for a moment or even a lifetime. But it does not need to be a competition or a pornographic experience. When sex is good, it's really good, but sometimes good enough is good enough.

Sex is a fantastic joint endeavour that can go wrong or come to a halt for a variety of reasons. But there is a way back to good sex: there can be sexual healing, it can be recovered with new depth and meaning. Sex therapy, as pioneered by Masters and Johnson, is tailored to fit the clients and their particular sexual difficulties. It has been used successfully for over forty-five years and is a major part of psychosexual training. The exercises and their application are explained here.

There are additions to the basic programme for specific problems such as premature ejaculation, loss of erection, pain on intercourse and the inability to reach orgasm. There is also a series of exercises to be carried out alone, if necessary, in order to familiarise oneself with one's body and discover what gives one pleasure.

If skilfully applied and the couple have sufficient trust in each other to commit to it and to fully co-operate with each other and with the therapist, sex therapy is highly successful. Because sex is so personal and touches our deepest being, the professional boundaries and ethics must be strictly observed. Clients need to feel they can be heard with acceptance and without judgement. There must be no physical contact and no personal revelations from the therapist. Sex therapy needs to take place in a safe, confidential space with shared trust, respect and intimacy, rather like sex itself.

Working psychosexually can be very directive and explicit, with a strong behavioural element. Often the therapist is in the role of teacher and must be careful not to be perceived as abusive or exploitative. The therapist and the clients will be working in a very delicate, sensitive and personal area, often with material that may never have been talked about. Clients will have anxieties about the process being too invasive and revelatory. Often they need permission to share difficult feelings that may be perceived as unacceptable, shameful even. In turn the therapist needs to be informed, confident and sensitive and able to share those qualities with clients in a respectful way. I hope this is reflected in the way I have told some of my clients' stories, which are so meaningful and important, each in their own way.

Carol Martin-Sperry

CHAPTER ONE

Gone Off It

Too busy

Alex and Charlie were a young, energetic and good-looking couple who had not had sex for over a year and now they wanted to have a baby. But they had grown apart and did not know how to kick-start their sexual relationship. They thought they had it all – the romantic courtship, the glamorous wedding, the exotic honeymoon. They had bought a house and done it up, and they were ready now. But they barely had time to talk to each other. He was a financial analyst, she was a pediatrician, and they both worked very long hours. In order to manage their stress levels she went to the gym three times a week and he went running. They both came home late every evening and were often on their laptops. Meals were usually eaten in silence in front of the TV. Weekends were spent shopping for food, cleaning the house, doing laundry and ironing and other chores. They socialised a lot with their peer group and visited their parents once a month. Absolutely no time for sex – except on holiday. Their last holiday had been skiing with a group of friends and there had been a lot of carousing, but no sex.

Charlie and Alex looked at me expectantly. There was something a little naïve about them, I thought. I felt that they had romanticised their relationship and had not really come to grips with real life. They were not able to prioritise their sexual relationship – they were sharing their lives like flatmates, desire had gone out of the window. Sex does not necessarily take up much time. One can have a meaningful sexual encounter in under an hour. What was lacking here was attention and intimacy.

And so I gave them some homework – 'Try eating your evening meal at the table without the TV on; you could talk to each other about your day and show a genuine interest in what the other person is saying.' I also instructed them, 'No laptops or mobiles after dinner. By all means watch TV together, snuggle up on the sofa. Go to bed at the same time, have a non-threatening kiss and a cuddle, maintain some physical contact in bed – it doesn't have to be sexual.' They blinked and looked at each other; this did not seem too daunting.

'We'll give it a go,' Charlie promised tentatively. Alex nodded.

At the next session they reported back.

'We managed three evenings,' Alex told me.

'Not bad, next week make it five,' I said.

They came back and told me that they had completed the task four times.

'OK, what are the difficulties in doing this?' I asked.

They had found it very hard not to check their phones, which distracted them and led to other activities.

'Right, each time you slip up you have to pay a forfeit,' I said.

They liked that idea.

I had to get them each to take responsibility for themselves. Reminding them that they had not had sex for over a year and that they wanted to have a baby, I stepped it up.

'Make a date at the weekend – nothing too complicated, a walk or a film or a meal. Continue dating on a weekly basis, like teenagers. First, you hold hands, then you share a chaste kiss and then the kissing gets serious. Next, you are snogging and pretty soon she'll ask you in for a drink. Things could get heavy on the sofa! Are you both ready? And so to bed! This programme may take a few dates but that's fine, you are not in a hurry. It may sound corny and unspontaneous, but it usually works.'

They immediately saw that this could be fun, but I wanted them to move on from being adolescents to grown-ups. I suggested further ideas for them. Charlie could take Alex shopping for nice underwear and good perfume, and she could organise a weekend away. Or he could get tickets for a play or a ballet, while she might plan the next holiday. Of course they could improvise, but it was up to them both to be proactive and adult about their relationship – I could not keep telling them what to do.

By paying attention to each other and giving each other time, the love and intimacy between Alex and Charlie returned. Soon they were making love because the mutual desire was there again: they had rediscovered each other.

Too angry

Alan and Holly came to see me because they were having explosive rows. Anger is a difficult emotion to handle. When it comes to expressing anger, some of us are volcanoes and others are earthquakes. Holly was a volcano: there would be a big eruption with sparks, steam and lava, which was usually over quite quickly. But it was all out there to be seen. Alan, on the other hand, was more of an earthquake: everything seemed to be quiet, safe and reliable on the surface, yet underneath invisible forces were silently at work. Without warning the earth would crack and split open. This was followed by the uncertainty of aftershocks before the earth settled down again.

Anger can be experienced as overwhelming and frightening, or as something to dread. Volcanoes make a lot of noise and heat, but earthquakes mean one cannot even trust the ground beneath one's feet.

Alan and Holly were no longer having sex but they were having huge arguments. In the early days of their relationship the tempestuous rows led to reconciliation with wild sex. In fact they had been known to provoke an argument in order to get to the hot sex. It was very passionate and the drama kept the adrenalin going. Afterwards they would feel the calm that came with the release of tension. But over the years the angry confrontations reflected their power struggles and battles for control: they were at war with each other. Now they were having enormous rows about the most trivial issues such as household chores, but this symbolised bigger and more fundamental issues of which they were not aware.

They knew how to push each other's buttons and it would get nasty. 'You fucking bitch!' he would say, 'You arsehole!' she would shout back. This was followed by recriminations and eventually half-felt apologies. The rows no longer ended in lovemaking but in resentment and blame, with an accompanying feeling of emotional exhaustion and despair on both sides.

I asked each of them how anger was shown in their families:

- Did it lead to shouting and gesticulation, fights and violence, or days of silence and sulking?
- Was there one bad-tempered member in the family who was labelled the angry one, who did it on behalf of all the others?
- When you have an argument about something trivial, what are you really angry about?
- When you feel constantly angry with your partner, who are you really angry with?

- Who does your partner remind you of?
- Who are you really punishing?

Both Alan and Holly were the middle children of three siblings – all boys on his side, girls on hers. Holly grew up in a very expressive emotional family, with a warm but volatile mother who shouted a lot. She and her sisters were used to arguing and jostling for power. Her father, however, was somewhat cold and distant. Eventually her parents split up and divorced. Holly did not want to repeat their marriage by falling into the same familiar patterns of behaviour.

By contrast Alan's family did not show their feelings at all. His father was the dominant partner, his mother somewhat passive and submissive and actually quite depressed. It was a household that seethed and sulked, a fiercely competitive and manipulative family. Alan was sent to boarding school when he was eight and learned to repress his feelings . . . until he met Holly. He loved her for her extrovert, passionate personality and for enabling him to show his true feelings.

In therapy they worked out that Alan did not want Holly to be submissive like his mother, but that meant accepting her as she really was. Holly in turn did not want Alan to be remote and distant like her father, but she had to stop provoking him. They were taking their anger with their parents out on each other; they also needed to learn how to talk to each other and to hear what the other person was saying.

Anger leads to arguments, rows, conflict and confrontation. Avoiding conflict is often seen as a major task in relationships, yet healthy conflict is an important part of any relationship. Couples need to trust each other enough to have a row and come through it. 'We never row' is not a good sign. Real connection means feeling safe enough in the relationship to express frustration, anger and annoyance and come out the other side.

When Holly and Alan were in the middle of a row, they were not always in touch with their adult selves. Often they would behave like competitive, point-scoring, manipulative children or even furious and demanding toddlers having a tantrum. Sometimes they were in touch with the judgemental and critical feelings of a punishing parent and expressed their anger in an attacking way. In no way could this be conducive to a loving sexual relationship.

Good communication is essential to resolving rows. If they could talk to each other, actively listen and be heard, any issue in the relationship could be dealt with. This meant talking without blame or criticism, listening to the other without interruption and reflecting back what they had each heard. I asked if they could put the rows on hold for the moment and bring the issues to the consulting room, and then I gave them some guidelines for good communication:

- Not using 'should', 'could', 'ought', 'you always', 'you never'

- Taking responsibility for one's own feelings
- Keeping to the present, not bringing up past resentments
- Turning complaints and criticisms into requests
- Ensuring one's own expectations are realistic
- Being assertive, not aggressive
- Not being defensive
- Distinguishing feelings from judgements
- Knowing when to apologise
- Agreeing to disagree
- Giving to get
- Making it a win-win situation, so there are no losers.

Naturally, it was a lot to take on board. Both Alan and Holly found it hard to put themself in the other one's place with genuine empathy. Often they had different perceptions of events, but both were valid. When it came to negotiating, they needed to state clearly what was non-negotiable for each of them. I suggested they could bargain with reciprocity – 'If I do this for you, would you do that for me?'

They found the **ACT** formula was helpful:

Accept difference

Compromise wherever possible

Tolerate what cannot be changed

Sometimes one has to make **ACT** a **FACT** by adding:

Forgiveness and generosity

In other words if you can't change it, don't fight it: go with it and embrace the pain.

Good sex requires trust and intimacy. No one wants to make love when they are angry and resentful, or when they feel criticised and blamed. In an angry relationship sex is usually the last thing to get sorted out because forgiveness is an act of generosity and intimacy requires the rebuilding of trust in oneself as well as in the other.

Because Holly and Alan really loved each other they were committed to exploring their rows and attributing their anger to where it really belonged, not just to each other. Getting back to lovemaking took time, but the passionate connection they had in the beginning was still there. Managing their anger brought sexual healing.

'Don't hit me'

Ed and Rita both claimed to be emotionally and physically abused by the other. In fact the rows were so bad that Ed had moved out. He told me he had 'battle fatigue' and could not cope any longer. Rita said he had a problem with drugs and alcohol, which made him aggressive and volatile. He in turn accused her of provoking him and she threw that right back in his face. This couple certainly knew how to push each other's buttons. Throughout their first session with me they shouted insults at each other. It did indeed feel like a war zone.

Ed was a well-known TV actor who liked to party on drink and drugs. Rita was attracted to him because he was flirty and funny, generous and easy-going, but she added that he was also a shambolic, lazy slob whose life was chaotic, and his erratic behaviour and massive temper tantrums were driving her crazy. To me he sounded pretty self-centred and narcissistic at first, but I also saw that he really loved Rita, but that things had got out of control.

Rita was a musician who taught piano. In contrast to Ed she was a very tidy and organised person. He accused her of being 'a totally anal control freak', but he loved her because she was also caring, loyal and highly perceptive. I wondered whether she might be a little OCD. Certainly she remained very self-contained in the sessions, but I felt this was her way of protecting herself. They were both very hurt.

Their sexual relationship had been full-on and passionate until six months previously. So what had happened? Rita had had a miscarriage and sex had stopped. Ed got very emotional and tearful when she told me this. Rita was taken aback because the miscarriage had never really been talked about. She looked at him with an expression of great sadness and a single tear slid silently down her cheek. Clearly hurt, she was vulnerable despite her silence. Rita had been in denial about her feelings of loss and bereavement and Ed had gone on a massive drink and drugs binge immediately after the miscarriage.

The rows had got worse. He accused her of being 'passive/aggressive and manipulative', she told him he was 'an insensitive bully'. Then it got really nasty; he had pushed and shoved her, she hit him. That's when they realised they needed professional help.

Why all the destructive anger? Where had it come from? We talked more about the miscarriage and their shared disappointment and sense of failure. Together they were able to mourn their lost baby. Ed admitted he dare not make love to Rita in case he hurt her; she said her body had completely shut down. For both of them sex had become associated with death as opposed to being a life force that would make a baby. But I felt their anger was about something completely different. So what was it like, growing up in their respective families?

Ed revealed: 'My parents had terrible fights and were violent with each other. My father drank a lot and had a series of affairs – I think my mother was depressed as well as angry.' Their situation had scared him and so he had left home as soon as he could. Ed had wanted to be an actor so that he could pretend to be someone else. At drama school he took a lot of recreational drugs. He was lucky to get into television early on in his career, which led to him being a bit full of himself and very much one of the lads. It was easy getting girlfriends, but he did not fall in love until he met Rita. Now he was afraid of repeating his parents' marriage.

The anger in Rita's family was never shown; emotionally, they were a cold bunch. She too had a father who drank and a depressed mother, but nothing was ever acknowledged or talked about. There was a complex code of behaviour around feelings and emotions, a menacing atmosphere of manipulation and resentment while avoiding at all costs any outward conflict or confrontation. 'Sometimes I felt I was going mad,' she admitted. Unlike Ed, Rita needed order and structure to make sense of the inner unspoken chaos. She too desperately wanted a relationship that was different from her parents', but when Ed got angry with her she simply did not know how to respond until she felt that he too was driving her mad. Then she became defensive and withdrawn, which in turn provoked Ed even more.

We started to untangle all their angry feelings so that they could admit that much of their anger was to do with their parents, in particular their heavy-drinking fathers. Rita began to understand that her behaviour frustrated Ed because it confused him. Ed realised she had no idea how to express anger in a safe way.

Both Ed and Rita were emotional orphans in need of love and affection. Hurt and insecure, they wanted positive regard and recognition. Their anger prevented each of them from giving and receiving love. Both had to find a way to manage their anger. We agreed that they would stop insulting and blaming each other and would bring their disagreements and anger to the sessions. They then had to learn how to negotiate and compromise whenever possible. It was a struggle because both of them turned out to be very stubborn, but they understood something had to give and the rows must stop because their relationship was at risk.

Ed stopped drinking and taking drugs and joined a men's therapy group, which proved to be an eye-opener: he was not alone. Rita took up yoga and learned to relax and be less rigid, both physically and psychologically. As usual in relationships with problems, sex was the last thing to get sorted, but once they had forgiven each other and rebuilt the trust, they were very relieved to find each other again. Ed invited Rita away for a reconciliation weekend and she asked him to move back in.

And baby makes three . . .

Freddie and Alison were an anxious-looking couple who found it hard to talk about their difficulties. They had not had sex since the birth of their son Luke, now two. Freddie felt jealous and resentful; Alison felt he was unsupportive. They had frequent rows, which were destructive and abusive. There was neither trust nor intimacy between them. They said they wanted to accept their differences, care for each other and resume their sexual relationship, but they didn't seem able to make the first step. At first I instinctively felt I must be cautious with them because I was convinced they were deeply troubled.

Alison, thirty-seven, was a shop assistant. As she sat down in front of me and clenched her hands in her lap, she had a look of wariness about her. She told me she came from a large family that was ruled by a manipulative mother who shouted and hit her children. Alison felt emotionally abused and a victim of her parents' volatile relationship. It seemed to me that she also felt incapable of being in a trusting and loving relationship because she had so little experience of one. It took several sessions before she was finally able to open up.

Freddie was thirty-six and worked as a carpenter. He sat very stiffly with his arms firmly crossed in a defensive manner. He told me his family was cold and not emotional, and that the atmosphere was one of stultifying repression. His father was authoritarian and controlling. Freddie's mother had told him he was special but withheld affection. He sought his parents' approval but never got any praise in return. I felt he was very needy and quite desperate, but talking about his feelings was not something he had done before.

This was not a happy, loving couple.

Freddie and Alison's relationship had always been stormy but had worsened when Alison became pregnant. During her pregnancy Freddie found it difficult to be intimate. 'It didn't seem right,' he explained. Alison felt he had let her down during a long and painful labour – 'He just wasn't there for me, I was frightened and trying not to panic.'

Freddie had found the whole business pretty scary; he also felt jealous and displaced. Alison meanwhile had doubts about her ability to be a good-enough mother. Her husband was unable to support her since he grew increasingly envious of the attention his son was getting. Luke's birth was not a joyful event but a major crisis in the relationship. To add to Freddie's difficulties, his father died suddenly of a stroke soon after Luke was born.

'I felt very confused. I was happy about Luke but in shock about my dad,' said Freddie.

Celebration and bereavement do not go together.

Alison admitted, 'I was too exhausted to take much notice of him.'

They were both feeling lonely and unsupported.

When they first met, Freddie had been attracted to Alison's natural warmth and passion. She saw him as calm and strong. But then they discovered each other's hidden, darker side. Both were depressed and angry; they were also very needy and distrustful but unable to give each other any comfort or support when it mattered.

If Freddie and Alison could barely be a couple, how would they ever tolerate being a threesome? Freddie saw Luke getting all the love and attention that he had missed out on in infancy and was now missing again. He could not bear the pain of his frustration and envy so he took it out on Alison. She barely had enough emotional resources to sustain her son, let alone Freddie's needs. He threatened to leave her, which terrified Alison. This reminded her of being similarly threatened by her mother in childhood and she did not know how to cope with it.

After several months Freddie began talking about wanting sex – 'I still thought I'd be better off leaving her and finding someone else.' Alison was so scared of being abandoned that she now started listening to him instead of just panicking. Talking about physical contact revealed just how unlovable they felt – 'We both feel we are shit,' Alison said. She was so scared to give her husband a little of what he wanted, as he devalued it and made her feel she would never be good enough. He was still punishing her for giving her love to Luke.

I pointed out that sex was the one special thing that Freddie could have with Alison that Luke would never have. He and Luke both had penises; Alison needed to acknowledge that she could have Freddie's penis but not Luke's. But it was proving hard for Freddie to be in touch with his potency – what he really wanted was Alison's nurturing breasts and her mothering. It turned out that he was the one who was not ready for sex, despite what he had been saying. Because Alison had become a mother she was no longer a sexual being in his eyes and he needed her more as a mother than a sexual partner. Freddie was like an infant who did not get the breast when he needed it, resulting in overwhelming feelings of fear, anger, frustration, loss of trust and despair. Like a hungry baby, crying alone in a darkened room, he was also full of revenge and a desire to punish his partner for not looking after him.

Freddie and Alison were emotional orphans, which was partly why they were attracted to each other. It was by no means certain they could regain their sexual relationship until they could be, and feel, more adult. They needed to understand how their childhood experiences had affected them as adults before they could even think about resuming any physical contact. Making those connections was painful for them – this was deep stuff – but they listened and stopped blaming each other for the love that had been missing so early on in their lives.

It was hard work and a long haul. We worked together for nine months until they both felt confident enough to make love again. Eventually they were able to open up to each other in a more positive and trusting way, and they began to understand each other better. Only then were they able to find reconciliation and sexual healing.

Mother, madonna, whore

Paul came to see me on his own. He was in love with his partner but since she'd given birth to their daughter he couldn't make love to her. Amanda felt very upset and didn't understand why. She had got her figure back, the baby was just about sleeping through the night, surely they should be feeling happy now? Paul was confused: it was the first time this had happened to him and he didn't know how to deal with it. He would wake up with an erection and he was masturbating so the problem wasn't physical. Also, he adored Amanda and he was so proud of her: she was a good mother and the baby was thriving but he just didn't desire her anymore.

'Amanda was unlike any of my previous girlfriends – she was deep, she took things seriously. I admired and respected her for that. She wouldn't go to bed with me until we'd been going out for three months. She wasn't very experienced but I liked that – she made me feel special,' he told me.

Paul had been pretty promiscuous before he met Amanda. For him sex had been all about lust and pleasure, the thrill of it. Whenever he did a line of coke, it was mind-blowing, but he was ready to settle down now and he had put that lifestyle behind him.

After several months of erectile dysfunction he found himself contacting one of 'the girls' – he needed to know if he could still get it up. She set him up with a beautiful and raunchy Russian, and within minutes he was hard and inside her. So there was nothing wrong with him after all. Paul began sleeping with call girls on a regular basis: he was in control, he could get blow-jobs and anal sex, none of which he would dream of asking Amanda for because that was 'dirty' sex, and he could walk away with no emotional attachment. But he still felt guilty.

'My mum was a prostitute,' he told me, shame-faced. 'She died of a heroin overdose when I was twelve and I was sent to a children's home. Nobody wanted to foster a mixed-race boy. I had two brothers and a younger sister but we were split up. It took me years to track them down. We all had different dads – I never met mine. Amanda doesn't know any of this; she thinks my parents divorced and my mum died in a car accident. I'm too ashamed to tell her she was on the game – it's my dirty secret.'

With a background like that, no wonder Paul felt conflicted about sex. There were two kinds of women in his mind: nice, clean girls like Amanda, and hookers. Nice girls were pure, the kind you could fall in love with; hookers were for screwing. Only now Amanda had become a mother herself, which kind of confused things. Paul didn't want her to have sex, it didn't feel right; he felt he was protecting her. When he made love to her he used to fantasise about what he did with the girls but he just couldn't do that now. He was in a bind. His mother had been a prostitute; she had lost her innocence long before he was born. In his mind mothers shouldn't have sex, he couldn't make love to Amanda now that she was a mother, but he could have sex with prostitutes even though his own mother had been a prostitute herself. He realised for the first time that he was really angry with his mother, and having cold, loveless sex with call girls was some sort of revenge.

Paul needed to talk about his confusion and his attitude to women. He also needed to talk about his mother, whom he barely remembered. It wasn't going to be easy and it would take time for him to gain aware-ness and insight. He needed to accept that Amanda had transformed from being almost a virgin into being a mother and that her sexuality was transforming, too. Accepting her as a sexual being and as a mother did not mean she was like his own mother. He would have to explain a few things to Amanda without causing her terrible pain. Better not to tell her about the prostitutes, but he could tell her the truth about his mother and how this had led him to categorise women. Only then would he be able to have a loving sexual relationship with her.

Despite Paul's deep shame, he told Amanda the truth about his parents. She was shocked but compassionate because she loved him. This came as a great relief to him and proved to be a turning point in their relationship. He decided not to tell her that he had been seeing prostitutes. Sex with them had been all about lust, but now he was discovering that desire could come out of intimacy and love.

Insights from the therapist

As we can see from Freddie and Alison's story and Paul's experience, having a baby and starting a family is probably the single biggest transformation and change a couple will go through and it's irreversible – there is no going back. It's a time of emotional upheaval and psychological readjustment. Moving from being two to three or more meant they would never be a couple alone together until their children finally grew up and left home, by which time they would be middle-aged.

When a couple decide to have a baby, sex immediately takes on a different meaning and becomes something important and powerful as opposed to fun and games. If the woman doesn't become pregnant after several months, both partners can start to feel anxious and disappointed. Sex has to be planned at a precise time and may lose its spontaneity, joy and fun. It becomes a chore when you are both under pressure to conceive. Some women may succeed in getting pregnant and then suffer a miscarriage. Both partners then need to deal with the ensuing feelings of sadness and loss, as we saw in Ed and Rita's story.

Pregnant women are awash with hormones and feel their bodies changing shape, growing larger and rounder. They may feel more beautiful or they may just feel fat. Their desire for sex may increase, or they may not want it at all. Some men find pregnant women very sexy and desirable, while others, like Freddie, hardly dare touch them. They may fear harming the baby if they have sex, although this is extremely unlikely. Or they may see their partner as a sacred mother figure not to be sullied by sex, which is how Paul felt.

Childbirth is a big deal. However well prepared couples may think they are, no one can really explain the magnitude of this event, the shock to the system, the fact that life will never be the same again. Couples often have unrealistic expectations of the process and feel disappointed and let down if it does not quite turn out the way they planned.

Most fathers want to witness the birth of their child and be supportive to their partners. Although they are not part of the physical process of pregnancy and childbirth, they can share some of the emotions. But some men do not wish to be there: they are afraid of the blood and guts, of seeing the vagina in its functioning role, of witnessing such extreme pain. And they may feel useless, guilty even. A few will be put off sex because they cannot bear to put their partner at risk of having to repeat the experience of childbirth.

This is what Freddie told me: 'I was horrified by what Alison went through. After twenty-two hours I was shattered. Then it all started happening. They had to use forceps. It was gruesome, I felt quite sick. She made these terrible noises; I was in tears. I felt so guilty – because of me she had to go through this. Then my son was born and my wife was so thrilled and happy. I just felt bewildered; I hadn't enjoyed any of it.

'When we got home the baby was on the breast all the time, for weeks on end. Of course I couldn't say it but I felt she had turned into a cow. She didn't want to make love, I felt rejected; we both went completely off sex. It was a very strange time.'

Alison's breasts, once his alone to touch and fondle, were no longer objects of desire. They were swollen, painful and functional, devoted solely to the needs of the intruder. Her intimacy and attachment were now primarily focused on the baby.

Since men are excluded from the physical process of pregnancy, childbirth and breastfeeding, they can't be expected to fully understand what their partner has experienced. While Alison needed support, encouragement and reassurance, who was there to give that to Freddie? He was no longer her number one priority, the centre of her universe; he had been displaced. Some men find it hard to bear and escape into work or even have an affair. Freddie thought of leaving.

Meanwhile Alison was forced to deal with at least a year of surplus hormones and a body that would never be quite the same again. Whose body was it – hers, Freddie's or the baby's? Was she a mother, partner or worker? After giving birth many women lose their sense of identity and sense of self; they no longer know what their role is. Huge demands are being made of them. The freedom and independence they once took for granted are replaced by major responsibilities, even a feeling of being trapped.

Alison said: 'After my baby was born I felt every cell in my body had changed, from the roots of my hair to the tips of my toes. I knew I would never feel the same again. From now on, my life was determined by "before" and "after".

So how can new parents find the time and energy for their relationship? With some difficulty, it seems. Will they ever have sex again? Yes, but maybe not for a while, or even a long while in some cases. The sexual relationship may need rebuilding. They now know that sex has its consequences. She may not lose the extra weight she has put on for several months; she could also be recovering from a Caesarean or a particularly difficult birth, which may have affected her both physically and psychologically. He may now see her as a mother and not as a sexual being, which is what happened to Paul. But it's not all doom and gloom. There are just as many women who have easy births, get their figures back and want to have sex again after a few weeks. They maintain their self-confidence and adjust well to their new circumstances.

IVF treatment

Charlotte and Peter, who were in their late thirties, had been trying for a baby for seven years. This included four failed IVF treatments and now Charlotte wanted to go for a fifth attempt. The doctors had told them there was nothing wrong with either of them, but this just left Charlotte feeling angry and frustrated. She was used to being in control of things and she expected this to work out – but it hadn't.

'I can't imagine not having a baby, not being a mother. My life would be meaningless,' she told me.

The couple had talked about adoption, but Peter had said he didn't want to bring up another man's child. They had both gone off sex but they never talked about it. Now Peter did not want to go ahead with yet another IVF attempt, but Charlotte was completely obsessed. In the sessions they were not really listening to each other, although I did my best to reflect back what I heard.

'I just can't go through the stress again. I'm sick of looking at tacky photos and masturbating into a test-tube, I'm sick of her mood swings and I just can't cope with any more disappointment and failure. The last few years have been very difficult and have put a huge strain on us. She's completely obsessed about it. I think we've got to come to terms with not having a baby – it's not the end of the world, we have a pretty good life,' said Peter.

But it *was* the end of the world for Charlotte. 'You just don't understand,' she told him, repeating in a desperate voice, 'I *want* a baby, I *want* to be a mother!'

While Peter got used to the idea of not being a father, Charlotte sulked. They stopped having sex altogether. One day Peter remarked on this. The next day Charlotte told him she wanted a divorce. He was shocked; he was even more shocked when she told him she had met someone else who was prepared to try IVF. Her obsession had ruined her marriage. But that was not the end of the story: Peter was actually quite relieved not to be under constant pressure. He eventually met someone else who loved him for who he was, not just as a sperm donor. Within a year she was pregnant, although they weren't even trying.

Charlotte had two more IVF attempts with her new partner, who had proved his fertility by having two children already, but she never did have a baby. Instead she had to settle for being a stepmother.

Couples who fail to get pregnant and turn to IVF are not always clear about the chances of success or failure, or what they must go through. There are various procedures available, most of which involve endless blood tests and powerful hormone injections with strong side effects that include severe mood swings. These are followed by a surgical procedure to harvest the eggs, a sperm sample, the test-tube fertilisation and the placing of the embryo in the womb. The woman may become pregnant, but this is frequently followed by miscarriage because the embryo fails to implant. So you start all over again, as Charlotte did.

It's a gruelling process in the best of circumstances. Couples need to function as a team in the face of anxiety, disappointment and loss, often accompanied by anger and despair and, finally, feelings of failure and shame. It's all too easy to apportion blame and to feel guilty. The sexual relationship is bound to suffer in this situation. Medicalisation of conception is so far removed from the natural process of making love that sex may seem irrelevant, and yet there may be some comfort in the closeness of intimacy as this difficult time is shared.

Celibacy

Bob and Sally were having no sex at all and wanted to explore the reasons why. They both felt a bit guilty about it. I found them remote in the sessions – neither was particularly communicative so it was hard going.

Sally was tall but I had no idea about the shape of her body because she wore dark, loose clothing that hid her figure. Her hair was scraped back in a ponytail and she wore little make-up, if any – she looked like an anxious little girl. She had grown up in a family with three generations of abuse. Her grandfather had sexually abused both Sally and her mother, her uncle had abused her and so too had her brother. This was a seriously dysfunctional family with few sexual boundaries. Making use of her and her sister was the norm. Her father, in a desperate attempt to protect his daughters, sent Sally and her sister away to a convent boarding school. Unfortunately this proved to be a harsh and punishing environment where the children taunted each other and the nuns were spiteful and cruel. Sin loomed large on the daily curriculum, bodies were dirty, menstruation was never talked about; touching oneself was both dirty and sinful, as was any sexual contact. As a consequence, Sally left school with a very poor body image, low self-esteem and a feeling of deep shame. She associated any form of sex with sin and guilt.

As a result of her history of sexual abuse and ignorance about her body, combined with the brutal reaction of the nuns to anything sexual, Sally had completely shut down her sexuality. She felt she had no right to pleasure and she had no ability to fantasise about sex. Sex filled her with fear. She also had difficulties with trust and intimacy because she herself had never experienced either.

Bob was also tall and somewhat dishevelled. He grew up on a farm deep in the country. His mother had a drawn-out cancer and died when he was six years of age. He had an older sister, but they were not close. His father was very hardworking and remote. There were no hugs and cuddles in the family and sex was never talked about. When he had wet dreams, Bob washed his own sheets. He had no girlfriends at school because he was so shy and awkward. His only sexual experience was a one-off mutual masturbation with a boy from his class, which left him feeling unclean and guilty.

Bob and Sally met at college in a small town, following which she became a legal secretary and he worked in IT. Both lonely emotional orphans who did not socialise easily, they shared a love of long country walks, rock climbing and birdwatching. They had a quiet wedding and were both virgins when they married. It took them a few nights before they felt able to have sex. It was awkward and painful; he came very quickly, she found it messy and disgusting and experienced flashbacks of the sexual abuse she had suffered. There was no real connection or pleasure and they soon gave it up. Both had had unloving parents and suffered neglect; neither of them wanted children. They had never experienced unconditional love and they held back emotionally as well as physically, careful not to hurt the other. On the whole their lives were quite content – they enjoyed each other's company even if they kept some distance from each other.

Bob and Sally came to see me to explore the possibility of having a sexual relationship since they both felt under pressure. We started with very simple sex therapy exercises (see chapter 2) to help them explore their own bodies before exploring each other's, but this was soon abandoned as they were not really motivated. In fact they were actively resistant to exploring sex and eventually I realised that the status quo actually suited them. So, was it a cop-out? It was not for me to attempt to impose a sexual relationship on them – celibacy could be a valid choice. There was a sense of relief when I suggested that they could choose to abstain from sex. They found it liberating now that the pressure was off and they could share inner calm and spiritual peace. The simplicity of this solution was that the whole problematic issue was taken care of. It suited them, even though it might be contrary to my basic thinking about sex.

***

Colum and Bridget were also in a celibate marriage but this time the outcome of our sessions was quite different. She came from a large, warm Irish family that she was still very much attached to. Her six siblings were still in Ireland, she was the one to leave and she missed them. They were a very religious family and Bridget was a fully practising Catholic, who worshipped the Virgin Mary and prayed to her every day. Her mother had told her when she got engaged that sex was a marital duty to be endured for the sake of having babies – that was the extent of Bridget's sex education. She had given birth to three children in four years and now she did not want any more. Birth control was out of the question. Anyway sex had served its purpose, which was the procreation of children, so she did not see the need for it now. It was not a pleasurable activity for her. Somehow she expected Colum to share her rigid views.

He too belonged to a large Irish family, but they rowed all the time and he could not wait to get away, which is why he had left home as soon as he could. Colum had a rebellious nature that Bridget did not understand. He would have stopped going to Mass, had Bridget let him. While she had repressed her sexuality in the context of her understanding of Catholic doctrine, he had repressed his feelings because of his avoidance of conflict and confrontation. Both were quite immature in their different ways. Sex or the lack of it had never been talked about – it was too embarrassing. Neither felt appreciated by the other. Colum perceived Bridget as controlling and possessive while she wanted him to be more involved in family life. He felt the children took her away from him, she believed his work distanced him from her. Neither was getting the warmth they expected. She would provoke rows with him, he would retreat, and this only made her feel more neglected: they were in a vicious circle.

When Colum confessed in a session that he was having an affair, Bridget was horrified – he was an adulterer, he had to go. She would never divorce him because of her faith, but actually she was relieved to see him go. Bridget moved back to Ireland to be close to her family and chose to remain celibate, which in a strange way felt empowering to her. After all, he was the sinner, not her.

Insights from the therapist

Desire, which is both an instinct and a drive, is subtle and complex. To one degree or another it engages all five senses: sight, touch, hearing, taste and smell. As individuals we are each turned on by our own particular combination of the senses. However, desire is more than just sensation. There are environmental, emotional and psychological factors as well as physical. We know that it is controlled by the brain and therefore affected by our thoughts, our feelings and our fantasies. Desire responds to physical and psychological stimuli. Positive messages to the brain will enhance desire, whereas negative ones simply shut it down.

As individuals we are all different. We need to know what turns us on, what turns us off, what engages the brain and what disengages it. The brain is our most erogenous zone. As we learn from our sexual experiences, it is helpful to share this deeply personal information with our partner. It's good to share our thoughts and feelings, maybe even explore some of our fantasies together.

Human beings have differing levels of desire, differing sex drives, just as they have different appetites, different levels of hunger. The only way through is compromise to avoid getting into a vicious circle of pressure and rejection, anxiety, anger and hurt.

Desire can be fragile and many factors will affect it. Illness of any kind will most likely have some effect on desire and performance. Gynaecological, urological and sexually transmitted infections all need medical attention and are inconducive to having sex.

One client told me: 'I got painful attacks of cystitis after making love. It was like peeing through burning razor blades. I ended up avoiding sex altogether. Luckily my GP gave me a pill to take after sex and that stopped it.'

The list of conditions for women, whose reproductive system and sexual organs are more complex and more at risk than male ones, includes:

- Miscarriages, abortion, childbirth, episiotomy, uterine prolapse
- PMT, endometriosis, menopause, hormonal imbalance
- Polycystic ovaries, blocked fallopian tubes, fibroids
- Cancer of the cervix, ovaries, uterus, breasts
- Haemorrhoids, cystitis, stress incontinence
- Sexually transmitted infections
- Thrush, vaginitis, pelvic inflammatory disease.

For men, problems include:

- Foreskin problems
- Prostate problems, cancer
- Urinary infections

- Hormone problems
- Sexually transmitted infections.

One client revealed: 'When I got gonorrhoea I was too embarrassed and ashamed to tell my ex-girlfriend until the clinic told me what could happen to her. It put me off sex for a while, I felt so guilty. Now I use condoms.'

Sexually transmitted infections (STIs) need to be taken seriously with a visit to a specialist clinic for tests and treatment. Some of these conditions are symptomless in women and can even lead to infertility. Here are the main ones:

- Herpes
- Genital warts
- Chlamydia
- Fungal infections
- Gonorrhoea
- Syphilis
- HIV/Aids.

Other conditions that can affect levels of desire are:

- Injury, accident, trauma, surgery, pain
- Abuse of drugs, alcohol, cigarettes.

Clients have revealed the following during our sessions:

'My partner was involved in a serious car accident. She was shaky for weeks after that. She wanted cuddles but she just didn't want to have sex.'

'My GP didn't tell me that the anti-depressant she had prescribed would affect my levels of desire. I felt much better but I lost interest in sex for a while.'

Many commonly used prescription drugs may have side effects that can affect levels of desire, sexual response and performance. These include:

- Blood pressure lowering drugs, cholesterol lowering drugs
- Anti-depressants, tranquillisers, anti-psychotics, neuroleptics
- Corticosteroids, the contraceptive pill, HRT, other hormone treatments.

For pre-menopausal women contraception is essential at all times unless you are prepared to risk pregnancy. All forms of birth control may affect desire and sexual response in some way. Unfortunately the perfect, trouble-free contraceptive has yet to be invented.

External events such as bereavement, family difficulties and problems at work may cause loss of desire, as will anything that creates stress and fatigue. For example, 'My partner's mum died of cancer – he was heartbroken. I thought sex would cheer him up but he couldn't touch me for weeks. He said my body made him think of her. It was so sad but I just had to be patient.'

Then there are personal problems such as depression and low self-esteem. Family messages about sex, spoken or unspoken, may leave us with inhibitions and rules about what is acceptable and what isn't. Sally had body image issues because of her history of abuse, which in turn left a legacy of fear and anxiety. Bridget came from a religious and cultural background, which left her with feelings of guilt and shame.

There may be a fear of intimacy and commitment, like Freddie and Alison experienced – 'We've been arguing a lot. I feel I'm the one that has to give in most of the time. It's put me right off sex, I'm just too angry with him.'

As we saw with Alan and Holly and Ed and Rita, conflicts, power struggles and battles for control in the relationship will be a major factor in killing off desire. Feelings of anger and resentment will affect desire and may cause you to withhold sex. This can be a powerful way of punishing your partner, whether consciously or not.

Lack of time also appears to be a major reason for loss of desire. These days people lead such busy and stressful lives that they no longer prioritise their sexual relationship. Alex and Charlie simply couldn't find time for sex.

The stories in this chapter show that desire cannot be taken for granted. Often it is a mystery, which is also part of its appeal.

CHAPTER TWO

Technical Difficulties

Faking it

'I've been with Tom for two years and I've faked it from the start. Now he's proposed to me and we're getting married next year, and I can't go on pretending. It's not fair on him and it's dishonest. What am I going to do? I've been living a lie all this time!'

Lisa was a pretty young woman who wanted to please everyone because she was insecure and she thought this would bring her the attention and affection she needed. Also, she wanted to impress Tom with her sophisticated sexuality, but the reality was that although she quite enjoyed sex, she had never had an orgasm, and she was too embarrassed to tell him. She was also scared that he would finish with her if he found out the truth. She'd talked to her best friend about it, but the conversation had not been helpful – it had just made her feel even more inadequate. Everyone else seemed to be having mind-blowing orgasms but she did not even know what that really meant. Her sexuality seemed to be under wraps.

Lisa grew up in a Catholic home with a disapproving mother. She had had no sex education at all apart from some very basic biology at her convent school. Her body was a mystery and she had had no incentive to find out about it until now. I suggested she should start discovering her sexuality by completing a series of sex therapy exercises on her own so that she could find out more about her body and her responses. Up to 70 per cent of women do not have orgasms through penetrative sex alone, I told her. Lisa was surprised and relieved.

'The first exercise helps you to get more acquainted with your body. You may also learn new things about how your body looks and how subtly it works; new things about how your body feels when it is touched, especially in places you hadn't thought of before. When you feel familiar with your body, you will then be more able to feel real pleasure,' I told her.

'Set aside approximately thirty minutes when you will be alone and undisturbed. You need a full-length mirror and a hand mirror. Try to clear your mind of worries and responsibilities in order to focus on what you are doing. You are going to start by taking a warm bath or shower but this is not just to get clean. If bathing, experience it in a new way. You may like to use some bubble bath and light a scented candle. Lower yourself slowly into the bath and concentrate on how the different parts of your body react to the wetness; be aware of the feel of the warm water on your skin. For example, it may feel quite different on your legs to how it feels on the small of your back. If showering, turn around under the shower and let the water hit different parts of your body. Experiment with different water pressures but never directly inside the vagina. How does it feel as the water strikes your shoulders, stomach and arms? Now soap yourself, using your hands or a flannel. Try both. Be aware of different textures on your skin. Are there other ways of feeling good? Do some areas feel good in a relaxing sort of way, while others are more energising? Be aware of the sound of the water too.

'When you have finished your bath or shower, concentrate on how it feels to dry yourself. Try patting gently, then rubbing hard. Which does your skin prefer? Allow yourself to really experience the drying process, don't rush it. Out of habit we often focus on just the main parts. Spend some time on the other parts of the body, such as your ears, hands, fingers and toes.

'Now stand in front of the mirror and notice the overall shape of your body. Pay attention to what you are doing; it may not be easy at first, and your mind may wander. If that happens, simply bring your mind back to the task. Study your body. Try to look at it from all angles, using a hand mirror to get a good view of your back. While your face will be very familiar to you, your body may be less so. Notice its asymmetry. See what hair distribution there may be; this varies from person to person. We all have some on our bodies. Sometimes there is hair surrounding the areola (the dark area around the nipple). It can also extend up from the genital area towards the navel or down the inner thighs. How do you feel about this? What about your pubic hair? Is it sparse or quite bushy? Both are normal.'

Women are often inhibited about their bodies because of scars or stretch marks. Stretch marks are very common and frequently occur around the hips, stomach and legs, whether or not you have had children. Most people start off by noticing what they don't like about their body: their breasts are too big or too small and so on. Often we pick up ideas on how we ought to look, but in reality we are all different. If, however, you feel that you are seriously under- or overweight, you might be prompted to do something about this. Bear in mind that often we cannot change the way we are, whether naturally skinny or curvy.

Back to Lisa ... 'Now ask yourself, what have I learned from this exercise? What have I noticed or discovered about my body that I didn't know before?' I continued. 'You may want to repeat this exercise a couple of times before you become familiar with the way you really look.'

After listening carefully to what I had to say, Lisa agreed to try the exercise, although she wasn't entirely convinced, for it seemed too simple. However, when I next saw her she admitted that the task I had set had been interesting. She had never been curious about the different parts of her body in this way.

Her next task was to touch herself all over: to feel the different skin textures not just of her limbs and torso, but also her face, breasts and genitalia. I gave her instructions for the following exercise, which is less clinical and more sensual.

'Start with a relaxing bath or shower as before and, while drying, remind yourself of the things you have learned in the first task. Use the sensitivity of your fingers to notice and appreciate the varying textures of your body. Start from your head and slowly work your way down. Be really aware, almost as if you are touching your body for the first time. Take your time; remember to breathe. Let your hands run over the features of your face, linger on the lips, inside as well as on the surface. Look at and touch the front of your body, notice the feel of your skin. Explore your hands, arms, shoulders and breasts. Now move your hands slowly over your stomach, let them run through your pubic hair, inside your thighs, over your legs, then your feet and toes. Relax as you do this and value your body even if you are not what you consider to be an ideal shape. Become aware of the different textures and notice how each part feels. Which parts do you enjoy touching and what sort of touch do they most respond to? Concentrate on what you are doing and try not to let your mind wander. If it does, simply bring it back to the task. Keep breathing!

'The first time you do this it might feel rather strange or even uncomfortable. For many of us there are long-established taboos about touching our bodies and especially noticing sensations of pleasure and arousal. After the second or third time you can let your hands explore further over your breasts as you touch them. You may notice your breasts and nipple size change. Your breasts become firmer and your nipples may become erect. Run your hands over your pubic hair again and over your genitals; become aware of their shape and texture. Sometimes use a dry hand and other times use oil, lotion or talcum powder to enjoy the different sensations and responses of your body.

'Again, ask yourself what have I learnt from this exercise and what have I noticed or discovered about my body that I didn't know before? Repeat several times.'

'Wow, so many variations!' Lisa said when she next saw me. She was beginning to enjoy this journey of exploration. Getting to know her body intimately was helping her to find out what felt good, which kind of touch she found pleasurable. I was pleased that she was showing no resistance; on the contrary she was very motivated, which made it easier for us both.

We moved on to the next task, which was to familiarise herself with her genitals.

'This exercise is intended to encourage you to experiment and explore further, physically and sensually, and to learn more about what, where and how you enjoy being touched. For this you will need a hand mirror,' I explained.

'Always start with a relaxing bath or shower. Slowly work through the first two stages – this will help you to relax and will reinforce the bits you feel comfortable with. Now prop yourself up against something firm, like a headboard or pillows. Bend your knees and open your legs to expose your genitals. Position and prop up the mirror so that your hands are free and you can see your genitals.

'Start off by looking at, and touching, your pubic hair. Note again how it is distributed, where it starts and ends; also its texture. This hair is necessary because it protects the very sensitive part of your body from friction, irritation and perspiration. Now move onto your genital lips (or labia). The outer lips are also covered by pubic hair for protection. Identify the outer and inner lips, the inner being smaller than the outer ones. You will need to use your fingers to pull the lips apart to see them properly. No two women are alike and the variation in size and shape can differ noticeably from woman to woman. Sometimes the inner lips are more prominent and hang down between the outer lips. The colour of the lips also varies, so note your size and colour. Feel the lips and notice the difference in their texture.

'You will have to pull the lips fairly wide apart to expose your vagina, urethra and the clitoris. Usually the inner lips meet at the top of the clitoral hood, the bit that protects the clitoris; the urethra is between the vagina and the clitoris. When you have found them you can look for the anus and the perineum (the muscle between the vagina and the anus). Often the clitoris, which is a woman's most sensitive part, is difficult to find since it is protected by the clitoral hood, and in an unaroused state it may be withdrawn and hard to locate. There are considerable variations in the size of the clitoris.

'Now let your fingers explore and feel around the mouth of the vagina. Do this stage slowly. Initially just feel around the lips, the clitoris and the vagina, and take your time. When you feel OK about it, let your fingers very gently explore further and feel inside your vagina. Try to identify the ridges on the inner walls. Notice how the texture changes as you feel further inside. The vagina is usually moist but occasionally dryness can occur (you may like to use a lubricant to do this exercise). You may become aroused during this exercise and that's fine. Notice how the clitoris becomes hard and erect, how the labia change colour and the vagina becomes moist.

'When you have finished this exercise, take your time, relax and think about it all, especially the new things you have learned about your sexual response. As before, it is useful to repeat this exercise several times. And remember, there is no goal to achieve an orgasm.'

Lisa was very enthusiastic when we met for our next session.

'Gosh, it's complicated! But I think I've worked out what is where. It felt very good down there,' she said. She was losing her inhibitions and allowing herself to feel pleasure.

'Excellent!' I told her. 'Now you're going to do it all over again and allow yourself to become really absorbed in touching your genitals, particularly near or on the clitoris. Be gentle; take it slow and easy. Check that you are relaxed and breathing well. Try and get into a day-dreamy state, visualise whatever makes you feel good sexually with your partner when he kisses and touches you. Start fantasising. This is about developing your sensuality and giving yourself pleasure. There is still no goal for reaching orgasm. Chase away any negative thoughts or feelings of anxiety. Give yourself full per-mission to be doing what you are doing. You are alone and in charge, no one is watching or judging you.'

Lisa repeated the exercises several times and was really enjoying herself. Sometimes she got very aroused, other times not. I asked her to think about what made the difference. Then one day she told me excitedly that she had felt a distinct, very pleasurable series of flutterings and a warm feeling in the pit of her stomach. Now she was on her way, it was time to go shopping! I suggested she should browse the Internet or visit a sex shop to buy a vibrator.

She came back to me with two different-shaped ones and some batteries and we had a good laugh as she switched them on and tried them on the inside of her arm, where her skin was quite sensitive. By now Lisa was very aware of her responses and much more con-fident about her body. Most women will reach orgasm with a vibrator applied to the clitoral area and she was more than ready.

'Wow! I can do it!' she told me when I next saw her. I felt really pleased for her. Now she had to bring her partner into her secret. I suggested that she told him that sometimes she didn't want penetrative sex but she would like him to touch her genitals in certain ways. She could guide him to the right place and tell him what kind of strokes aroused her. This worked a treat and he soon learned how to touch her clitoral area as they made love. He was only too pleased to see that she was interested in enriching their lovemaking. After a while I asked her how she felt about oral sex. This had been a taboo area, but now that she was so familiar with her body and her responses she felt confident enough to ask for it. And of course it blew her mind. His too!

This inhibited and embarrassed young woman had come a long way and was now able to enjoy a fulfilling, satisfying and varied sex life, thanks to the programme of self-discovery exercises. She had given herself permission to masturbate and I had helped her learn the skills.

The female orgasm is mysterious. Orgasm in women is a series of contractions originating in the clitoris with its myriad nerve endings, and it can be felt as anything from a tiny local butterfly flutter to powerful river-deep, mountain-high uterine contractions that ripple throughout the body. Some women are multi-orgasmic – this means that their arousal levels can return more than once to the plateau phase and rise again to orgasm. By contrast, some women have had plenty of sex but have never experienced an orgasm.

As for the disputed G spot, it is usually situated in some women on the wall of the vagina. The latest thinking is that it is made up of very sensitive clitoral nerve-endings which, when stimulated, can trigger an orgasm.

The majority of women are not orgasmic with penetrative sex – they need manual or oral stimulation beforehand or during lovemaking. Many women enjoy the experience of sex without coming. Most women will reach orgasm with the use of a vibrator on or near the clitoris.

Why do so many women fake orgasm? Some feel they have to prove just how extremely sexy they are, or how very skilled their partner is. Some need a lot of foreplay time but don't ask for it. Many more still believe that women are supposed to have orgasms from penetrative sex, or, even less likely, every time they have any kind of sex. There is a lot of media and porn pressure to perform and moan the house down. Once you start faking, it's very hard to stop because it means being honest and owning up to deception.

It's best to know your body and its responses and not be goal-oriented. Just relax, go with the flow and let go of your thoughts. Be fully present in the moment, aware of all the many sensations. Some women reach orgasm simply by imagining they are going to have one. This is the power of fantasy.

Useless prick!

Jack and Ellie had been together for two years. Their sex life had never been very imaginative and Ellie had remarked on it. Jack felt humiliated but had not known how to deal with it. After a few months he had developed erectile difficulties and was avoiding sex. There was nothing wrong with him physically but in Ellie's eyes he was a failure and he felt blamed and ashamed.

Jack had been attracted to Ellie, who was very beautiful, because he thought she was warm and loving and would give him the intimacy and affection that he had lacked from his mother. Sadly this was not to be. Ellie turned out to be similarly hostile and rejecting. She wanted a strong man who would admire her and put her on a pedestal, which Jack had done when they first met, but now he could not satisfy her.

Jack was a disappointment to his mother because she had very much wanted another daughter. From the start her feelings for him had been ambivalent. When his younger sister was born, she had no time for him anymore and he was sent straight off to full-time nursery school. As the middle child, he was more or less left to get on with life on his own. Both his sisters ignored him and he got little attention from either parent. His father was a withdrawn, undemonstrative man who was actually quite weak, and his mother was aggressive and critical. A cold, hard woman, she walked out on his father as Jack turned eighteen and was leaving home for university. Her parting words to her husband were that he was a 'useless prick'. For Jack, these words struck home.

Ellie's mother was demanding and manipulative. She was jealous of Ellie, who was close to her father. He in turn adored his daughter and spoilt her, but he could not stand up for himself (Jack's penis could not stand up for itself). His passivity with her mother really irritated Ellie. She could not understand why he stayed with her. Both Jack and Ellie were repeating the same patterns in their parents' marriages: they had strong, difficult mothers and weak, ineffectual fathers in common. Both had thought their relationship would be different.

In therapy, Jack was able to recognise the recurring patterns, but Ellie became increasingly hostile and defensive. Just as his mother had emasculated his father, so Ellie had emasculated and shamed Jack with his sexual inadequacy. He had identified with his father, the 'useless prick'. No wonder he could not achieve or maintain his erections.

Eventually Ellie realised that she would have to take responsibility for her attitude and make some changes. She had to admit how disappointed she was with her father's weakness and let go of her fantasy of being extra-special to him. And she was frustrated because Jack had also failed to make her feel extra-special. She blamed his erectile problems, but would not admit that she herself was part of the problem: Jack needed her to be more sensitive and caring, but he also had to stop identifying with his own father.

Instead of being dragged down by a vicious circle, Ellie and Jack had to start building on a positive circle. From believing they had an identified sexual problem, they understood that it was more of a psychological and emotional difficulty, as is so often the case when sex goes wrong. There was a lot of work ahead of them and both had to forgive the other, which required generosity. Once they understood how their parents' marriages had affected them and that they did not have to repeat those behavioural patterns, they were able to make changes. They followed a programme of exercises (see page 57) and grew much more confident about their sexual encounters.

Insights from the therapist

There are times in every man's life when he just can't get an erection, or else he has an erection and then loses it. It happens, it's just one of those things, no big deal. However, if it is happening too often or on a regular basis, it becomes a problem and it's worth doing something about it. Most women, however understanding, will often feel rejected or blamed in this situation. They may question their attractiveness or their sexual performance and lose confidence and self-esteem. She will need him to reassure her that he still finds her attractive and desirable.

When sex goes wrong it can become a vicious circle. Fear of failure brings on performance anxiety. You may avoid sex altogether rather than get it wrong, which can lead to humiliation and guilt, rows and anger. There are feelings of failure on both sides and the relationship can become fraught.

Impotence is a blow to most men. It is literally a loss of power. Men can feel useless and worthless; also confused, frustrated and embarrassed. So much is invested in the erect penis that it's not surprising it doesn't always rise to the occasion. It's important not to get caught up in a vicious circle of pressure, anxiety and disappointment.

First, you need to check for physical causes. Do any of the following apply to you?

- Diabetes
- Cardiovascular problems
- Multiple sclerosis
- Accidents, trauma or injury
- Low testosterone levels
- Long-term use of alcohol and nicotine.

If so, you need medical help. It's worth talking to your GP about erectile problems, especially if you are on any medication.

If you wake up most mornings with an erection and if you get an erection when you masturbate, the problem is more than likely to be psychological rather than physical. Here are just some of the other factors that can contribute to erectile difficulties:

- Anxiety
- Stress
- Depression
- Exhaustion
- Work problems
- Family issues
- Bereavement
- Low self-esteem
- Body image
- Gender identity.

You may have a fear of commitment or of intimacy. Perhaps your deeper feelings about sex are conflicted. You may feel ambivalent about your relationship. Are you angry with your partner? Are you still attached to your mother at some level? If you haven't separated emotionally, the incest taboo may unconsciously come into play and sex is affected.

Here are some practical guidelines for overcoming the problem, as I discussed with Jack:

- Agree that you are not going to have penetrative sex for the time being, but can have physical and sexual encounters
- Say no when you are not in the mood
- Only initiate sex when you feel like it
- Make sure you are relaxed and not feeling anxious
- Check out your partner's expectations
- Make sure your conditions for arousal are being met and that you are getting the right kind of stimulation – it's personal.

Viagra has now become a generic word. There are newer and faster drugs today, such as Cialis and Levitra. Do not buy them off the Internet as they may be adulterated; go to your GP for a prescription. There is no benefit in using them recreationally. These drugs work by controlling one enzyme that acts on a second enzyme, which in turn expands the veins in the penis and allows the increased flow of blood into the penis to form an erection. They do not work unless there is desire and a signal from the brain to release the first enzyme, though.

These are the exercises that helped Jack regain his erections: 'Masturbate until you have an erection. Now stop, let your penis grow soft. Start again. Do this twice in a row – you can use visualisation and fantasy. If this isn't helping, identify your negative thoughts, feelings and fears and explore them before you try again. You need to repeat this exercise at least four times over a week or two.

'Next, you are going to get physical with Ellie. Be touchy-feely, hold hands, put your arms round each other, share hugs, cuddles and kisses but no sex. Kiss, stroke and caress each other in bed. Don't be concerned with your penis: if you happen to get an erection just acknowledge it and let it go. It may come back; it may not, no matter. Stay relaxed, have fun and enjoy the sexual encounter.

'After repeating this exercise several times and when you feel ready, let your partner touch, stroke, rub, lick and suck your penis. Remember, there is no goal for an erection, but it may occur. You may need to repeat these exercises several times over the weeks, with no attempt at penetration.

'When you feel confident and relaxed about your ability to get an erection you can start doing the exercise, as follows. After the foreplay that you need, she sits on you and guides the tip of your penis into her vagina – it doesn't matter if you lose your erection, try again next time. After a few times of this you can take control yourself of inserting the tip of your penis.

'When you have followed these exercises to the point where you are confident about your erection you will both be wanting penetrative sex.'

These intimate exercises will only be effective in a loving and caring relationship with mutual honesty and trust. Jack and Ellie talked at length with me about their difficulties and were able to communicate more generously with each other. Despite a few hiccups along the way, Ellie co-operated with Jack during the exercises and eventually they found themselves making love in a less goal-oriented way.

An outing

Malcolm came to see me because he had problems maintaining his erection. He was a young man of thirty, who had been with his partner for two years. She had told him that the problem was his, so he must sort it. I felt this was a simplification and wondered what her part in it might be. He told me he could masturbate when necessary and he tried not to think of his shrinking penis.

Malcolm was a tall, slim, intelligent-looking man who worked as a research scientist for a pharmaceutical company. His story was not dramatic: he had an older sister who was married with a baby, and his parents were still together, although he believed this was more through habit, convention and passivity than anything else. Malcolm had grown up in a small town – 'very boring' was how he described it. When he got into Oxford he had looked forward to meeting like-minded people. He had worked hard and gained a good degree but somehow he never felt truly connected. It was the same with his work colleagues. He had met Fiona, who was a management consultant, when she was attached to his company on a project. She had a huge network of friends and managed their busy social life but there was always something missing.

For him sex had never been wonderful and he felt disappointed. He had lost his virginity rather awkwardly during the first term at Oxford. After that his sexual encounters followed a pattern. With the help of a couple of drinks he was at first keen and eager, but as soon as he was inside a girl, his penis would soften. The few girls he got that far with were generous on the whole and he found other ways of satisfying them, if not himself. Malcolm felt that everyone was having more sex and better sex than himself.

He did a bit better with Fiona, but when they moved in together at her insistence, the old problem returned and she was quite cross with him. Unaccustomed to being confronted, he also felt guilty and upset. He started to avoid sex altogether.

Was Malcolm's difficulty down to a problem with commitment, perhaps a fear of intimacy? He genuinely longed to be in a warm and loving sexual relationship but it just wasn't happening. Did he have issues separating from his mother, an unconscious fear of incestuous sex? Apparently not. What sort of a role model had his father been? Typical of his generation, he had enjoyed a bit of sport, pints at the pub, loved a country walk and chats about politics.

I asked Malcolm to describe to me in detail what happened during his sexual encounters. Nothing unusual, but somewhere there was a block. I then asked how he had learned about sex. Nothing from his parents, it seemed, although his sister hadn't spared him. Friends at school had jostled and jeered in the changing room and he had joined in half-heartedly. He did have a crush on an older boy, but apart from a few mutual masturbatory encounters nothing ever came of it and besides he was not the only one.

I asked Malcolm about his sexual fantasies. At this point he shifted uncomfortably and would not look me in the eye. I gently persisted. He gave me some very ordinary and unimaginative answers, which I suspected were untrue, but I could not push him – he had to come out with it himself.

Finally, it did come out and *he* came out: Malcolm was gay. Admitting this was traumatic for him, but there could be no other way. He would have to tell Fiona, which would be very painful for them both. His sister was not surprised but he could not face his parents.

Initial shock and ambivalence gave way to a huge sense of relief. Then he realised he would have to find his way in a whole new world. This was very difficult for Malcolm for he was far too shy to hang out in gay bars and the idea of cruising the Internet was threatening. But he found the answer: at work he applied for a position which would take him to a different town, where he could be truthful about his sexuality and make a fresh start at his own pace. He felt both nervous and excited about this life change but it seemed the only way forward and I wished him well.

Love hurts

'We are trying for a baby, but we're hardly having any sex.'

Susie had always experienced pain on intercourse. She also suffered from chronic thrush, which she self-medicated because she was too embarrassed to talk to the doctor about it. The couple generally used condoms, which made Susie's thrush worse, but this was a problem they had not discussed. Duncan never complained, but she felt guilty and disappointed about the lack of sex in their marriage.

Her previous relationships had never lasted more than a year because of the sexual difficulties. Sex was less painful when she had had a few drinks, but she never really enjoyed it and had never had an orgasm; she did not masturbate. She had had a miscarriage in the previous year and was still very sad about it.

Feelings were not shown in her family and sex was never talked about. Susie was close to her mother and described her father as 'distant'. Her mother had given her very negative messages about childbirth and had told her that 'doing it' was something you must put up with if you wanted a baby. No wonder Susie had sexual difficulties.

Duncan's family were competitive and argumentative with high expectations of achievement. Professionally, both his father and brother were highly successful. An anxious and nervy person, he felt he had not done well enough and this had affected his self-esteem. He also felt guilty and disappointed about their sexual relationship – 'I'm really sad about the miscarriage too but I didn't talk about it because I didn't want to make Susie even more upset,' he explained. Then he added that in order not to hurt Susie he ejaculated as quickly as possible on the rare occasions when they did make love. He admitted that he had always done so and his previous relationships had ended because the sex was unsatisfactory and had come to a halt.

Susie was amazed when he told her all this: the problem was not hers alone. Together they mourned their lost baby and shared their hopes about having another one. We explored their loss of self-esteem and feelings of failure.

Sex therapy started with a mutually agreed ban on sexual intercourse to take away any pressure, anxiety or expectation. Although they weren't having sex in any case, this was presented as a verbal contract and both seemed relieved. I suggested they do self-exploratory exercises on their own to really familiarise themselves with their own bodies. We looked at the emotional climate in both their families and what gender and sexual messages each had received. Hers were about pain and his were about rapid achievement, which was reflected in their sexuality.

One of the more common sexual problems in young men is coming too quickly, premature ejaculation. This means not recognising the cut-off point of ejaculatory inevitability, the moment when you cannot prevent it from happening. It can occur before penetration, at the moment of penetration or after just a few thrusts. Most men like to be able to last longer and to have some kind of control about when they ejaculate. As I explained to Duncan and Susie, there are two techniques that can help overcome this problem.

'The stop/start method means masturbating, focusing on your penis and learning how to recognise the point of no return, the moment to stop just before you ejaculate. It takes practice – after all, you are learning new habits. Try to do this exercise about three times a week. Eventually you should be able to last for around fifteen minutes with two or three stops.

'The next step, when you are confident you are gaining more control, is to get your partner to masturbate you with the instruction to stop as and when. Keep doing this on a regular basis. Now you are ready for penetration. Lie back and let your partner sit on top of you. She can insert the tip of your penis and not move. When you can do this without coming she can insert your penis fully and not move. Be aware of how it feels. Try doing this lying side by side, then try with her moving while you lie still and you control your thrusts and she doesn't move. Eventually you should be able to have penetrative sex with both of you moving and without you coming prematurely. Don't attempt to do these exercises all in one go: it may take weeks. That's OK, keep at it – it's worth the effort.'

When Duncan and Susie felt ready, we moved on to shared exercises without any sexual goals, allowing them to really explore and discover each other's bodies at leisure. These involved spending equal time touching each other all over while engaging the senses and being focused and aware. I gave them mindful breathing and relaxation techniques too.

Eventually they felt ready to move on from the sensual to the sexual. First, I asked them both to practise masturbating on their own. Duncan was to notice the point of no return in his ejaculations, while Susie was to familiarise herself thoroughly with her genitals, inside and out. Now that they were on a good learning curve, the next task was to masturbate each other to orgasm. These tasks were repeated until they both felt motivated and confident enough to move on. It took time and patience, which was exactly what they needed to learn sexually.

Full sexual intercourse took a few goes but they were having fun and really enjoying themselves in the meantime. Eventually arousal and desire took over and Duncan and Susie were successfully making love. Now they could think about making babies.

Daddy, don't go!

Amanda suffered pain when she attempted to have sex, and two relationships had ended because of her sexual difficulty. The first man had called her a 'freak' and the second one had left her feeling a failure, convinced she was unattractive. She had not wanted sex with either of them but did not know how to say no. Her body had said it for her.

While growing up, the sexual messages in her family were very negative. Amanda's mother had had two miscarriages before Amanda was born and always told her daughter that another pregnancy would have killed her. Her parents had not had sex since her birth because her mother had experienced sex as literally life-threatening. Amanda's understanding was that sex was dangerous.

Her parents had divorced when she was ten but Amanda was still daddy's girl until he met Jean, four years later. She knew that Jean and her father were having sex. Amanda felt betrayed, he saw much less of her and she perceived this as almost an infidelity. When the couple were married a year later, Amanda was so angry and jealous that she refused to attend the wedding and cut herself off from her father. She blamed him for the loss of their special relationship. For her sex was not only dangerous, it was also destructive, and so she carried on in a lonely cocoon, avoiding relationships but safe from pain and rejection.

Amanda needed to reclaim her body as an adult and forgive her father for abandoning her. She also needed to understand what her mother's experience had been like and to know that she herself did not have to repeat it. She had a lot of growing up to do.

I suggested she start off by seeing a gynaecologist for reassurance, then we began working with self-focus exercises, which I explained to her.

'You need to find the best ways to relax and then to start exploring your genitals slowly and gently, perhaps in the bath or shower. When you feel confident enough, try inserting the tip of your finger with lots of lubrication. Keep repeating this exercise over the weeks until you can get your finger in without experiencing pain. Then try two fingers. Practise clenching and releasing the muscles round your vagina. Remember to relax and breathe; you are the one in control of your body and your vagina. Fantasies and visualisation may be helpful. Take your time, there is no rush.'

For women in a relationship the next step is to do these exercises with your partner and his finger. Next, try his thumb, then two fingers and eventually the tip of his penis as you sit on top of him. Don't forget to use plenty of lubrication and make sure you are fully aroused before you try complete penetration. These exercises require patience and understanding but are well worth it.

Amanda repeated the exercises until she felt comfortable with her genitals and was able to introduce first one finger into her vagina, then her thumb, then two fingers. She also learned to masturbate successfully. Soon afterwards she contacted her father and arranged to meet him. She apologised to him and later to her stepmother. Though she did not have a boyfriend yet, she felt much more able to have a relationship and was looking forward to sharing a positive sexual experience.

When sex hurts, the problem is very often psychological. It's easy to get caught up in a vicious circle of anxiety and fear following a painful experience which then leads to anticipation of pain, tension and further anxiety.

Daddy's little princess

The eldest of three children, Vicky was the apple of her father's eye. She was a pretty blonde, blue-eyed child who grew into an attractive and rebellious teenager.

Her father had brought her up to believe that she was special. His relationship with her was flirtatious, but controlling. Vicky did not get on with her mother, who was 'plain and submissive', but unconsciously she felt frustrated that, try as she might, she could not win her father away from her mother. This wasn't a sexual love – that would have been incestuous, which was wrong.

At the age of twenty Vicky fell in love with an older, married man. Aware that she was a sexy-looking young woman, she used seductive and manipulative behaviour to capture him. Part of the attraction was his initial unavailability and the illicit nature of the affair. Though eventually he got divorced and she married him, the union did not last long once the honeymoon phase was over. Vicky's manipulative use of her sexuality was in vain. The irony was that she did not actually enjoy sexual intercourse and penetration hurt because at an unconscious level it felt wrong: she was still in love with her father.

Vicky hated being on her own. She soon found a second husband who seemed more appropriate, but once he had fulfilled the basic function of providing her with two children, she grew bored with him. The sex became increasingly unsatisfactory and she started to treat him more like a brother. Eventually they too got divorced.

Vicky gave up on marriage and took a series of lovers, who were all older men. One by one she discarded them when the romance and the hot sex (faked) wore off, as they inevitably did. Each time her heart was truly broken, for love hurt in more ways than one. Throughout her relationships Vicky always turned to her father for help and advice so he remained the principal man in her life. He bailed her out in times of trouble and made all her major decisions for her. No wonder she was in love with him. Vicky never really grew up and was barely aware of her father's controlling influence. She seemed doomed to repeat her mistakes. Her partners could not compete and Vicky remained perched on the lonely pedestal her father had built for her.

After his death she had to come to terms with being alone with no one to rescue her. Through therapy she finally gave up on her fantasy of the knight in shining armour who would rescue her and she started to grow into her adulthood. Only then was she able to be in a satisfactory relationship and to start to enjoy sex without pain.

No entry

Natalie was a thirty-one-year-old virgin who suffered from vaginismus. This meant that penetrative sex was not possible for her because her vaginal muscles would go into involuntary spasm whenever anything came near. It's an unusual but distressing condition, something I had never come across in thirty years of practice, but I like a challenge and I immediately felt that I could work with Natalie. I felt sorry that this slim and pretty young French woman had been denied the pleasure of sex and I really wanted to help her overcome the problem.

Natalie was very nervous and embarrassed but she got straight to the point by telling me that she hated her genitals and couldn't touch them directly. She washed herself with a flannel and had touched herself lightly through the fabric of her underwear, but generally she felt disgusted with that part of her body. Although attractive, whenever she felt anxious or depressed she was convinced that she was ugly. She was completely disconnected from her body.

Natalie had had a few unsatisfactory adolescent experiences of kissing and petting which she had not enjoyed, and an on/off five-year friendship with a boy that eventually became sexual. Intercourse was not possible for her and he ended the relationship.

She met Gérard online. The relationship developed slowly, and after seeing each other for three months, it got physical. She told him that she liked having her breasts stroked but did not want him touching her vagina. They tried to have penetrative sex but were unable to do so. However, she did not mind giving him oral sex. One night he put his finger in her anus and eventually they started having anal sex, which she found quite pleasurable. I was surprised to hear this and asked why she felt disgust for her vagina but not for her anus. She said that her genitals were too complicated and hidden and she had never felt curious about them. As a child in France she had been treated with suppositories when she was ill and she associated her anal passage with healing.

Natalie continued to be very nervous when she talked to me, often avoiding eye contact. She said her thighs went numb and she had unpleasant tingling in her arms and legs. Sometimes I could see she was shaking. She was tense and on the edge of panic attacks. There was an infantile side to her, which she readily admitted. I assured her that we would proceed very gently and that I would not ask her to do anything she didn't want to. She was courageous in telling me her story and I felt quite touched by her predicament. I was pretty certain she was suffering from long-term post-traumatic stress.

Natalie had developed a breast cyst and went to Paris for a mammogram. Her mother sent her to a woman gynaecologist.

Natalie wept as she told me: 'I was petrified and ashamed but I told her I was a virgin. The doctor said I was suffering from vaginismus – I hate that word! She suggested I try inserting tampons but I can't even touch myself.'

It sounded as though the doctor had been very insensitive and Natalie was quite traumatised by this visit.

Now she feared any physical contact with her boyfriend. She was dissociated from her body and had desexualised herself. However, she was still extremely motivated and determined to solve her problem.

I asked if she felt ready to carry out an exercise, which was to touch her genital area with her bare hand with no pressure applied. She agreed.

At the next session I asked her what she thought her vagina was for. 'Having babies,' she replied. Her fear was that it was too small, too narrow, just a slit with no hole – a baby couldn't possibly come through it. She also saw it as ugly, too hidden, too complicated; something that couldn't be seen and now had to be explored, although she had never looked at it or felt it. It was not for putting things in. Natalie was also worried that her hymen would be pierced and torn and was surprised to learn that she might have already lost it. She was also concerned about infections. Her pubic hair was 'ugly' (I explained that it had a protective function, to prevent friction), the outer labia were just about OK but she couldn't touch her inner labia because they were too sensitive. She did not know where her clitoris was, so I drew a quick sketch of the inner and outer labia and located the clitoris, urethra, vagina, perineum and anus. I suggested that she might look at the American artist Georgia O'Keeffe's flower paintings online because they were beautiful representations of the female genitalia and could help to counteract her negative image of her vulva.

Natalie did the touching exercise three times, once in the bath where she felt relaxed, once with Gérard, and once on her own. To her surprise she had felt a certain amount of pleasure but she had also felt very anxious. This had expressed itself in an unpleasant tingling in her hands and forearms. As she described her experience to me the tingling reoccurred. She was a very sensitive young woman.

The next step was to touch her inner labia. I also asked her if Gérard could look at her genitals and describe them to her. She said that part of their foreplay was for her to open her legs and show him her genitals but he wasn't to touch.

Natalie had used a lot of negative vocabulary in talking about herself and her body, admitting she felt dissatisfied in general with herself. I had to be positive and encouraging, questioning some of her self-critical statements. At the beginning of the next session she told me that she felt less 'tortured', another strong word. I still wondered what might have happened to her in childhood. Natalie had looked at the O'Keeffe flowers with some interest, but I don't think she made a real connection. She had touched her inner labia and said that she found the texture 'strange', similar to what she thought was the entrance to her vagina. The experience had made her feel funny, vulnerable. She had felt anxious but managed to calm herself. Gérard had described her vulva as 'cute, sweet, pink, like pieces of clementine'. Natalie made the association with forbidden fruit. She told me that the exercises were easier when Gérard was there because he motivated her, but she did not understand why the sight of her genitals excited him, although she quite liked the feeling of his tongue on her vulva.

This young woman was having oral and anal sex but lived in fear of her vagina and said she could not bear to look at her genitals in a mirror. Natalie still felt scared and emotional but she was also beginning to feel intrigued, curious. She was making real progress and so I suggested that she should repeat the exercises whenever she could and ask Gérard to touch her in the same way.

Natalie wondered if she had some message from her father about marriage and virginity, although this was never said explicitly. She described her father as 'very strict and authoritarian' – she was not allowed to date or bring boys to the house and the message about any kind of sexual activity was that it was absolutely forbidden. And she was told she was 'untouchable'. Her father once hit her violently for smoking. She has always been afraid of him although she says she loves him. He seems to have been a distant, austere and forbidding presence in her life. Her mother used to hit her with a belt. She seems to have few boundaries and shares all her family and emotional problems with Natalie, including doubts about her husband's fidelity. She shouts and cries and blames her daughter for her woes, which in turn makes Natalie feel guilty. Natalie says her mother is a victim of her father's tyrannical behaviour.

These abusive parents had terrorised her and Natalie was angry with them. No wonder her sexuality had never developed naturally and her vagina had clamped shut.

'My parents are pretty crazy. I told my mother I was in therapy because of them – they have killed off my body,' she said. Then she told me she had no memory of her childhood before the age of seven. For me this rang alarm bells. What had happened that she had to forget? All she could recall was a nanny and a story her mother told her about being sexually attacked in an elevator. She could well have been sexually abused, but of course there was no way I could suggest this.

Natalie still did not want to touch herself but managed to do so with Gérard's encouragement. She certainly couldn't face looking at her genitals with a mirror – 'No! Too disgusting!' Natalie thought of her vagina as a source of pain and refused to believe it could ever give her pleasure. She couldn't believe her finger could enter it, let alone his finger or penis. Haunted by her fears, she said that she had no right to pleasure. Often she sulked or felt hopeless, then she would become strong and determined again. She knew she was immature and childish, but growing up and separating emotionally from her parents was very hard for her. Sometimes she was petulant and sulky with me but I held firm.

Then she had a dream about a beautiful garden that she couldn't get into. This represented her beautiful, closed-off body. I gave her more gentle exploratory exercises but she found excuses not to do them. She said she was disappointed and angry with herself but still she put off doing the exercises. Eventually she managed to repeat the touching exercises and was able to put the very tip of her finger just inside the inner labia. Then she went backwards again: she couldn't touch herself, it hurt. She could only touch herself with her knickers on, so I suggested she try from a crouching position. I suggested relaxation exercises but she resisted me and I had to be very patient. When Gérard tried to touch her, she couldn't open her legs. To help her relax, I taught her a sitting yoga position with her knees wide apart. I suggested she gave up wearing unattractive pyjamas in bed and sleep in a T-shirt, but she wanted to keep her knickers on. Natalie found it difficult to differentiate between the exercises and loving gestures. She felt threatened and pushed Gérard away and he in turn felt confused and rejected. Then one day she finally had the courage to look at herself in the mirror and she was shocked.

'My genitals are so ugly, like bits of bloody meat!' she told me.

But slowly things improved. I had to encourage her to repeat the touching exercises, the yoga position, to look at herself in the mirror again. She resisted, she was scared and she made excuses. When she did manage to look at her genitals in the mirror again it made her feel very emotional and she cried. We were making progress.

After six months she could touch herself, look at herself in the mirror and occasionally sleep naked next to Gérard. They had some cuddles. Eventually she allowed him to lightly touch her genitals, but then she backed off again.

'I just want to be left alone! You all have these expectations of my vagina, I'm under too much pressure!'

Natalie became very panicky, saying she felt assaulted and abused. She wanted to hit herself, pull out her hair. What had happened to this poor child? Was I pushing her too hard? She told me how she becomes disconnected from her body. When she feels stressed her body shuts down. She was literally out of touch with her body but she told Gérard she needed his help: she wanted him to kiss her and stroke her. He could touch her vagina from behind. One day he gave her very gentle oral sex and she felt aroused.

During one of our later sessions she told me that she liked her labia now and could touch herself, but the idea of penetration filled her with self-hatred and anger. She was frightened of being raped because of what her mother had told her. Sometimes when Gérard tried to put the tip of his finger in her vagina she would cry and cry. Although she had no childhood memories of abuse, I was certain she was silently working through something momentous which I was sure would help her move on, even though it was as yet unnamed.

We had been going on for a year by now. Natalie and Gérard had attempted penetrative sex from behind or with her on top but they didn't get anywhere. She wanted lots of sensual foreplay but she still really didn't want anything inside her as she was afraid it would hurt. For weeks they avoided physical contact because she was scared of failure, but then she felt guilty and would cry.

We discussed the use of tampons and I showed her one before and after putting it in water. Though shocked, she was prepared to give it a go with lots of lubricant. I asked how she felt about dilators and she agreed to try them, which surprised me. Meanwhile Gérard managed to insert his thumb an inch or so and she got her own finger in a little way and moved it in and out. This was huge progress and we both felt positive.

Natalie ordered the dilators online and brought them to me. We opened the box together. There were four smooth tapered plastic wands graded in size with a shield round the blunt end to stop it disappearing. She was shocked at the size of the biggest one, which was as big as a quite large erect penis. There was a DVD, which we watched together on my laptop. Natalie said the woman's vagina looked 'horrible'. Watching her insert a dilator, she was utterly amazed that it could slip in so easily. She was truly surprised and described it as 'surreal'. I suggested she try with the smallest one and lots of lubricant and see if she could keep it in for five minutes.

By now Natalie was very positively motivated; she had taken control of the situation and of her body. She managed to get number one and then number two into her vagina and hold it in for five minutes. Each time it took her thirty minutes just to get it in all the way and it 'hurt like hell' but she was so thrilled the first time, she called Gérard in to witness it.

I suggested she do relaxation breathing and try clenching and releasing her vaginal muscles. It took her a while to locate them but she did. She kept going with the first two sizes. Gérard treated her to a surprise holiday in the Caribbean, where he proposed to her. She started thinking she could have a baby. The following session she came to me with great news.

'I'm using tampons! It's fantastic, I don't have to use pads anymore!'

She was tremendously excited about this, and rightly so. I was very pleased.

Then she tried the number three dilator but it really hurt and so she went back to number two. On her next trip to Paris she confided in her mother about her vaginismus and her phobias. The following six months were spent organising the civil and religious weddings in France with the usual family tensions. Meanwhile Natalie was enjoying more sexual contact with Gérard and practising regularly with the dilators for up to half an hour each time.

Then she told me that the number three dilator was 'easy' and she could insert the number four dilator halfway without too much pain. Everything happened pretty quickly after that and very soon Gérard managed to fully penetrate her with no pain. It had taken two years but she had truly lost her virginity, just one week before her civil wedding.

That summer Natalie and Gérard moved to Paris because of work and I didn't see them again. Eighteen months later she emailed to tell me she was pregnant, and their son was born a few months later.

This was one of the most satisfying pieces of work I have ever done. Natalie overcame her terrible fears and phobias, and with Gérard's loving patience, understanding and support throughout her difficult journey with me she was able to change from a frightened little girl into a grown woman who could have a baby. I was so proud of her.

CHAPTER THREE

Infidelity

California dreamin'

Steve was forty-nine and three quarters and feeling bad about it. His bossy wife had coerced him into having a big party for his fiftieth but he was in no mood for celebrating. Recently he'd been diagnosed with cardiac arrhythmia and felt death staring him in the face, although his condition was perfectly treatable. His children were almost grown-up, work was becoming increasingly competitive and his marriage was running on empty. He'd given up going to the gym because he didn't like the full-length mirrors everywhere, and, to cap it all, he was losing his hair.

'This is my midlife crisis,' he said. It made him feel panicky and full of dread. But he couldn't talk to Karen about it – she'd only laugh at him and make some biting comment.

Steve paused as he told me his story; he seemed weary and defeated. I just knew what was coming next.

'And then I met Charmaine . . .' he said, giving me a sad look. Steve worked in management for a large chainstore and Charmaine worked in fashion retail. She was at least fifteen years younger than him, a long-haired, long-limbed gorgeous Californian, who maintained her looks and personal grooming to an all-American stand- ard. Steve was a sitting duck. This young woman was fully aware of her assets and knew how to use them to her advantage. She shined with confidence and can-do energy.

Steve was in love. Charmaine was not only beautiful, she was prepared to listen to him and share his prob- lems; she understood him. When they finally checked into a hotel one afternoon he couldn't believe his luck. She wrapped her long legs around him, pressed her pert young breasts into his chest and guided him expertly into her soft, moist vagina. The sex was fabulous – geni- tal, oral, anal, she was up for anything he asked for. She was just as efficient and caring in bed as she was at work. He was hooked. She knew he was married but she was playing a long game. The afternoon assignations became a regular feature and soon there wasn't a hotel in town that they hadn't made love in. 'I felt like a young man again,' he sighed.

Such a familiar story, only the personal details were different. I wondered how it would play out. Make or break?

Meanwhile, back home Karen had noticed that Steve was in a better mood and taking more care of his appearance. Their sex life had come to a halt because they were exhausted, busy, preoccupied and spent very little time actually being alone together. There was no closeness, no intimacy, but now she almost fancied him again and she made an effort to talk to him more often. Once she reached out tentatively to him in bed but he turned away from her. Oh well . . .

Months went by and then disaster struck. Karen could not find her mobile so she picked up Steve's and saw a text message that was not from her because it was definitely sexual and she would never dream of sending a sexy text. She felt herself burn with anger and shame. What a fool she had been, she almost wished she had not caught him out.

'What the hell is this? Who *is* she?' He was silent. She made him move into the spare room. He told the children that it was because of his snoring. They just said 'whatever', but he wondered what they really thought. It was a mess.

He told Charmaine what had happened; he could not bear to lose her. 'Oh, poor baby!' she cried, taking him in her arms, 'I love you, I'll look after you – she'll calm down.'

But Karen did not calm down. She shouted at him and called him all kinds of things. Then she cried for a week, and then she threatened to divorce him. They were on an emotional rollercoaster. Weeks turned into months. He carried on seeing Charmaine because he was in love with her. Paradoxically the sex with her made him feel safe – he could not envisage making love with Karen now, and Charmaine made no demands on him.

Karen wrung her hands and asked him to choose between her or 'that bitch'. But he did not want to make a choice because that meant losing one or the other. The status quo suited him; 'he was having his cake and eating it,' Karen said. But Steve was not happy; in fact, he was miserable.

In the end Charmaine told him, 'This is going nowhere so I've asked to be transferred back to Los Angeles. They're promoting me and I'm leaving in a couple of weeks.'

'But I love you,' a devastated Steve protested.

'Not enough to leave your wife; you'll get over it!' she told him. And she was gone, taking her youth and her beauty and sexuality with her.

What was he left with? A broken marriage, the end of his dreams, an ageing body and an increasingly shaky career, and he was in mourning not just for the gorgeous Charmaine but for his younger self. It was time to look in the mirror and accept that half his life was over and he had to make the most of the second half. Love, sex, who knew what lay ahead? He hoped Karen would one day forgive him but he knew it would take a long time.

'You didn't listen'

Mark and Kate had been married for twenty-one years. They had three teenage children and busy professional lives. Kate was a senior manager in HR for a big multinational; she had worked part-time when the children were small. Mark was a partner in an architectural practice which was struggling. They used to have an au pair but now their only domestic help was a cleaner.

The couple had very little spare time and both found it exhausting, running the home and managing their adolescent children, who were all facing exams. Their social life was minimal. 'We spend our weekends recovering from the heavy demands of the week, doing household chores and trying not to be grumpy and stressed-out,' Kate told me.

With three small children it had been difficult finding time for sex, and although they were sexually compatible and really enjoyed making love, it had now dwindled right down to holidays only. Mark was more upset than Kate about this lack of sex but somehow had not managed to talk about it; she did not seem to notice. A long-term committed relationship may start with romantic love and passion and then strong feelings of attachment and intimacy, but at some point it needs to transform from the 'in love' honeymoon phase into the enduring 'loving' phase. This is when sex can often become dull and routine or simply fade away, as it had with Mark and Kate.

Kate had let herself go but she did not seem to notice. Mark had hinted as such; also that she was drinking just a little too much. Kate was taken aback and hurt when she heard him say this, but still they were unable to talk about their sexual relationship. Mark's firm was in trouble and he valued Kate's advice but she was too busy to listen to him. She hadn't acknowledged his concerns and he felt isolated and unsupported. Theirs was no longer a companionate marriage. Ironically it was at Kate's forty-fifth birthday party that Mark met Daisy, a work colleague of hers. Daisy was ten years younger and divorced. She was bright, full of energy and obviously attracted to him, which was flattering. When she left, she gave him her card.

Mark did nothing about contacting Daisy until a month later, after a particularly gruesome weekend with the kids bickering, Kate non-stop on her computer because of some work problem, and take-out pizza for Sunday dinner. He got in touch with Daisy on the pretext of wanting her professional advice. They met for lunch and Mark talked throughout, Daisy listened. They met up again the following week and lunch became a regular date. After a couple of months he was able to ask her out on a Saturday night because Kate was away at a conference. He knew he was about to do something dangerous but he had felt lonely and neglected for a long time. After dinner Daisy invited him back to her place and he stayed till two in the morning.

Sex the first time was a bit awkward. Mark arranged to see her again the following afternoon and they both took their time. It was good, very good. After that they would spend many of their lunch hours at Daisy's flat, making love. He didn't feel guilty, just relieved; he also loved the thrill of the forbidden.

The crunch came some months later when Kate borrowed his laptop because she had left hers at work – 'I could not believe what I found on his emails. I was stunned.' When she confronted him, there was little he could say. He refused to answer her many questions. She got panicky and told the children, who were wondering why she was always in tears. They were angry and confused.

Kate was furious and very upset. She insisted Mark move out in order to get his head straight, but then she discovered that he was still seeing Daisy. After a few weeks both women gave him an ultimatum: he could not have his cake and eat it. All three of them were miserable, the children were anxious; it was a huge mess. Finally, Mark agreed not to see Daisy any more, which was hard for him because he hadn't wanted to hurt her and he really missed her. But he realised his behaviour threatened to destroy the family. He moved back home but Kate was not ready to forgive him unless they went to couples counselling.

It took several months for us to work through all their issues. As always in troubled relationships, sex was the last thing to get sorted. No one wants to make love when there is so much hurt and anger. Rebuilding trust takes a long time and needs genuine remorse on one side and true forgiveness on the other.

What were the real reasons for Mark's affair? He and Kate had been drifting along for a good while. If it wasn't the children, it was their work issues. Neither had prioritised the relationship, they had no time together as a couple. Kate had let herself go but Mark didn't dare mention it – she was far too sensitive about her appearance. Meanwhile he had major problems at work. If his firm went down there would be serious financial implications; he needed not only her support but her professional advice as he was having to make several people redundant. She hadn't realised how bad it was because she simply hadn't listened and he had given up trying to talk to her. However, Kate still saw herself as the innocent party: he was the one who had been unfaithful, obviously it was his fault. It was very hard for her to accept that she had neglected him and must take some responsibility for what had gone wrong in their relationship. This was not about shifting blame or condoning what he had done but understanding what had contributed to his infidelity. Mark felt guilty and ashamed and was truly contrite, but could she trust him? Regaining trust is very hard once it has been lost, and Mark understood that he too had to pay attention.

I suggested they go out together once a fortnight and take it in turns to arrange it. 'Agree to ban laptops and mobiles from the bedroom too,' I added. When things got tense and a row was looming, they dealt with it in the therapy session. It was hard for them to let go of resentments. There was a lot of shouting and tit-for-tat accusations, but eventually they started talking without blame and really listening to each other. They allowed themselves to feel sad as opposed to angry.

Finally, we got round to sex; they were anxious. 'Don't expect to go from zero to a hundred miles an hour in one go,' I told them and suggested they should 'take time to massage each other in turn with no sexual goal'. They were reluctant at first because it raised issues of trust and intimacy, which of course was at the crux of the matter. After a few times they became less tense and more confident; they were beginning to trust each other again.

Then Kate suggested they go away for a weekend together. Mark was thrilled. I helped them talk about their expectations. Both were cautious but hopeful. As it turned out, they did not make love on that occasion but they did share some sexual experience and were able to acknowledge it as progress. A couple of weeks later one Sunday afternoon when all the children were out of the house, Mark asked Kate to go to bed with him. It was awkward for them both, but afterwards they were in tears from the sense of sheer relief: sexual healing was on its way! They were pleased to find each other again. Their relationship was wounded, they had paid a heavy price, but they understood that things must be different in the future and nurturing the relationship was a shared responsibility. Now they were moving in the right direction.

The last time

Catherine was a thirty-year-old with a big diamond ring on her finger.

'I'm getting married in three weeks' time,' she announced but she looked anxious. Was she getting cold feet, I wondered. 'I know I'm doing the right thing,' she added, 'but I feel so guilty.' She looked at me nervously. 'You will think I'm a terrible person . . .' I reassured her and asked why she might feel she was a terrible person.

'Ten years ago when I was at Cambridge I met Will. He was Dutch, from Amsterdam – we were both reading economics. I fell in love with him immediately; we were inseparable. It was a very intense relationship and the sex was wonderful, I felt so lucky to be with him. In our last term we were both working really hard for our finals. I hadn't even realised that two or three days would go by without us seeing each other. Then I saw him in a café with his arm round another girl; I was devastated. I went to his room that evening and confronted him. He said it was nothing serious, just a bit of flirting. But how could he? We were in love with each other! Then he told me that he felt too young to make a commitment and that he was going back to Amsterdam after his exams. I couldn't believe what I was hearing and I told him I never wanted to see him again, it was over. He was very upset and tried to talk me round but I stuck to my guns. I left Cambridge and went travelling for a year. I was so hurt and heartbroken that that was the only way I could deal with it.'

Catherine fell silent, then she took a deep breath and continued with her story. I figured she must have seen Will again.

'Six months ago Will friended me on Facebook. I felt a little pang in my heart but thought nothing of it. Matt and I were deep into wedding preparations . . .

'Then came the bombshell. Will had terminal cancer, with only a few months to live and he wanted me to spend twenty-four hours with him in Amsterdam. He sent me his mobile number and asked me to get in touch with him. In my head I knew it was the wrong thing to do, but in my heart I said yes. How could I say no to a dying man who had loved me? I didn't tell anyone, I just went. It was crazy, but I had to do it.

'He met me at the airport and I was shocked at his appearance. My beautiful boy was bald and grey-skinned, shrunken, just skin and bones. This was real – he was dying.

'He took me to a nice hotel. We talked about how we had left each other at Cambridge and he apologised for being so immature at the time. "But given my present situation, it was probably just as well," he added, almost jokingly. I was very moved. We had room-service supper because he was too tired to go out. Then he asked me if I would share a bath with him. This was something we had never done but I understood that he needed that closeness and intimacy now. We lay in each other's arms in the warm water and afterwards he took me to bed and made love to me with such tenderness that I cried and he did too. We feel asleep wrapped around each other and woke up smiling. I was so touched.

'Leaving him was the hardest thing I have ever done, utterly heartbreaking. I walked through the airport in a daze, I felt numb. At home I wept all night and then I told Matt that I was ill and needed to stay in bed for a couple of days. He was so solicitous and concerned, but I needed to be alone. Will emailed me to thank me for the healing I had given him. After that, silence. Several weeks later his sister rang to let me know he had died – I couldn't face the funeral.'

There was a long silence. I watched the tears slip down her face.

'I'm not even married and I've already been unfaithful to my husband. I can't possibly tell him, but that means I've got this terrible secret. It was so wrong of me, wasn't it?'

I assured Catherine that it wasn't a question of right or wrong and this was the final part of a long and silent bereavement. The end of her relationship with Will in Cambridge had been incomplete, unsatisfactory. She had granted a dying man his last wish, which was quite noble. Now Will was part of her past, her future lay with Matt.

Life is not all black and white. Sometimes it's not as straightforward as we would like it to be, moral choices are not always simple and clear-cut. This was one of those rare occasions when a difficult decision had to be made and Catherine had followed her heart. Yes, she had been unfaithful to her fiancé and yes, she was holding a powerful secret, but surely we all have secrets, even from those we deeply love and trust? Parts of us necessarily remain unknown to others because we are not just protecting ourselves, we are protecting them as well. The person she had hurt the most was herself.

Catherine seemed relieved and I wished her well. I felt like a priest who has heard a confession and given some kind of absolution, hoping the person finds peace.

Insights from the therapist

How do you define infidelity? What constitutes an affair?

Different people have different answers. Some may feel that if their partner watches porn, it's a form of betrayal. Others are just about prepared to pardon a drunken kiss at a party but obviously not a more sexual fling or a one-night stand. One definition of infidelity might be any emotional or sexual involvement with a third person. Does that cover Facebook, Twitter and Skype? For some a personal text, chat or email correspondence with another person is taken as a sign of unfaithfulness if it is flirty or if it has an emotional connection.

So, where do you draw the line? How do you define 'sexual'? A look, a word, a touch can all be sexual. Bill Clinton famously said, 'I did not have sexual relations with that woman' – but of course he did! In Middle America, where evangelism and chastity are so important, young people are having oral sex because somehow that doesn't count as sex. There's nothing in the Bible banning it.

There is a lot of hypocrisy when it comes to sexual matters, especially when one reads in the press that an estimated 40 per cent of people are unfaithful to their partners. If your partner has strayed, would you want to know? It's a lose/lose situation. Should she or he tell and suffer the consequences, or not tell and live with the unspoken burden of secrets and lies? Either way, it's going to bring distance between you.

One client revealed: 'I went away to a conference, got a bit drunk and ended up in bed with a woman. I felt very guilty when I woke up and even worse when I got home. Why did I do it? I was flattered that anyone else would want to have sex with me and I was weak. Do I regret it? Yes, and no. I wouldn't do it again. There's no way I'm going to confess to my partner though; that would be disastrous. But now I have this huge secret.'

What about the so-called 'French solution'? The marriage, social and family life are solidly protected but she or he may take lovers outside the marriage. This is never overtly acknowledged or discussed. Avoidance and denial are the chosen way of managing it and maintaining the status quo. Are these pragmatic arrangements selfish and amoral, or do they provide some sexual healing and a practical way of coping with the pressure of unsatisfactory couplings? The French of course feel just as betrayed and shocked by infidelity as anyone else, however sexually sophisticated they may appear to be.

Secrecy requires following certain rules, keeping everything separate emotionally as well as practically and taking care not to be found out. That means immediately deleting all compromising texts and emails, not posting anything suspicious on Facebook or Twitter, not leaving compromising credit-card slips or receipts lying around, covering your tracks at all times and making sure your lover is obeying these rules too. Deceit requires attention and discipline and is harder than it sounds, as both Mark and Steve found out. However well one manages secrets, by definition they exclude the partner and therefore create distance in the relationship.

Human emotions are complex and messy. When we stray from the straight and narrow we risk being hurt and causing pain. Life seems easier when everything is black or white, right or wrong, good or bad. We need to follow codes of social conduct and moral imperatives or else our lives will become chaotic and threaten the foundations of our families and society. It's natural to be attracted to other people at some time or another, but we don't usually act on it. But it's not just the fear of being found out that keeps us from straying, it's the commitment to monogamy and the person we fell in love with.

So what makes us say yes to an affair?

Affairs are not just a threat to any relationship, they are a sign there is a problem in the relationship, as we witnessed in the story of Mark and Kate's marriage. When there is a major problem inside, we are tempted to look outside. Affairs are often seen as a reason to end a relationship, the cause of the break-up; but an affair is usually a symptom of something lacking, something going wrong. The relationship can recover from an affair if the underlying causes are explored and understood and steps are taken towards change by both parties. A crisis is a painful way of crying out for help.

People are unfaithful for many reasons. It's not just about sex, although some level of sexual involvement is usually present. Some of the reasons include lack of attention and affection, not feeling understood or heard, boredom and a need for excitement.

The secrecy and danger of an affair bring risk and a feeling of excitement and naughtiness that goes with the thrill of illicit activities. An affair is also an escape into fantasy and 'what if' – it makes one feel alive, special. But the unfaithful partner is concealing, lying, betraying. There is a serious failure of trust, a degree of separation brought about by the holding of the secret, as well as the infidelity. The other partner is excluded from the secret. Owning up or being found out may have painful consequences. The betrayed partner will be devastated and will experience many confused feelings similar to bereavement – shock, disbelief, anger and sadness as well as a loss of self-esteem, humiliation and a sense of failure. Some even seek revenge, harbouring a wish to punish their unfaithful partner.

Karen could not turn to Steve for support and consolation in a time of crisis because she saw him as the cause of that crisis. When Steve's affair ended, he was experiencing feelings of loss, grief, guilt and sadness and could not expect support and understanding from Karen. This made it complicated but it wasn't as simple as innocent or guilty, victim or persecutor – Karen needed to take responsibility for her part in the breakdown of their relationship. Many people in her situation are outraged at this suggestion and proclaim their innocence, but we are not just saints or sinners, persecutors or victims.

Both Kate and Karen wanted to know all the details, the 'who, when, where, how, what, why?' This was a no-win situation. Hearing the information was painful, but not knowing gave rise to fearful fantasies. It also compounded the feelings of guilt in the unfaithful partners. When Mark had to make a choice, he delayed the process because one way or another his decision entailed inevitable loss. It felt less painful maintaining the status quo, however unsatisfactory. Continuing crises and drama keep the adrenalin flowing, and real change means facing up to one's imperfections and weaknesses.

Both Steve and Mark's relationships had to be renegotiated on a new basis. Guilt and blame went back and forth, emotions were on a rollercoaster. Eventually there had to be understanding and forgiveness and a period of rebuilding trust, commitment and intimacy. The problems in the relationships that led to the affairs needed to be acknowledged, owned and dealt with by both parties if they were to have a shared future, with no recurrence of infidelity. It's a daunting task that takes time: betrayal and loss of trust leave their scars long after the wounds have healed.

Some people say, 'If only we could go back to how things were'. But there is no going back, nothing can quite be the same again – the vase has been broken.

However well it is repaired, both of you will always know that it fell to pieces. The unique wholeness has gone forever. Getting over an affair is like a bereavement – you need time to go through the stages of shock, anger and sadness. Healing comes after resignation, acceptance and letting go. Forgiveness requires generosity; building trust is almost an act of faith.

Paying for a one-night stand

Bill, Nick and David had each all spent a night with a prostitute but their stories had different outcomes . . .

Bill and Harriet were in their early thirties and had been together since university. They had married when Harriet was pregnant with their first baby and quickly decided to have a second child.

Harriet was working part-time and juggling child-care with her mother and someone else's au pair. It wasn't ideal but she was a caring, hands-on parent and the children were thriving. Her marriage, however, was down in fourth place after the children, her work and the home. She and Bill had not made love since her second pregnancy, two years previously. Bill was bewildered – he adored Harriet and begrudged her nothing, but he had the normal sex drive of a man of his age and he was aching from frustration but he didn't feel it was ever the right time to bring it up because Harriet was always so busy.

One night after he had been out drinking with colleagues Bill sat in his car, feeling lonely, so he checked out an escort service on his phone. After choosing a girl, he went through the procedures – it was that easy. He met her at a hotel. Slim and well groomed, she was also friendly and efficient. They talked a little and then they had sex, any way he wanted it. The sex was good. He felt a huge sense of relief afterwards, but he also felt empty – she wasn't Harriet, his wife whom he loved.

He got in at 5 a.m. and Harriet just knew – 'You've slept with someone, haven't you?' She was so sad. Bill couldn't lie; he couldn't look her in the eye so he just nodded. She turned away from him in the bed, saying, 'We'll talk about it later.' But Bill couldn't talk and so they needed help.

In therapy Harriet told him how hurt and betrayed she felt. Bill in turn explained how rejected he had felt and told her he hadn't wanted to be unfaithful. Harriet felt this was a cop-out, and that he should have talked to her. Now they were both in tears. They were beginning to understand that when you truly love someone you have the power to really hurt them. Bill had not been able to tell Harriet that he felt trapped with the responsibility of parenthood and he really needed her. He was surprised when Harriet told him that she too felt burdened. It was a relief to be able to share those mutual feelings.

Bill showed genuine remorse and asked for Harriet's forgiveness. It was difficult rebuilding trust and intimacy but they were both motivated. Harriet began to understand that she had taken their marriage for granted. She agreed to take responsibility for the sexual relationship she had neglected for so long and managed to arrange for them to spend a weekend alone together. It was a start.

His night with the prostitute had left its mark, but, with time, both Bill and Harriet could move on.

***

Nick's night with a prostitute occurred during a foreign business trip but with a very different outcome to the story above. He got extremely drunk and had been picked up in his hotel bar by a seductive young woman. Nick was so naïve he didn't even realise she was a prostitute until they got to his room and she asked for the money upfront. By then he was half-undressed and aroused; it was too late to get out of it. How professional of her!

When Nick got home, he was eaten up by guilt and a terrible sense of shame. There was no way he could pretend that nothing had happened. He confessed to Diana because he could not manage his guilt. Diana was devastated – she could not believe that he had done something so appalling. She was outraged. Nothing he said helped her to understand why he had succumbed to his fantasy, because it had indeed been a fantasy of his: sex for pure lust with no commitment, anything goes, no consequences. He tried to explain this to her but it simply made matters worse. Diana was so angry, she wanted to hit him; she threw him out of the bedroom and made him take an HIV test.

Despite professional success as a solicitor, Diana's self-esteem was at an all-time low. She felt fat, ugly and middle-aged. In reality she was only 44 and a good-looking woman. She was confused and bewildered. Meanwhile Nick slunk around the house with his tail between his legs. What had he been thinking of? It had nothing to do with thinking, that was the problem. He and Diana had a good life together, and now it was broken. Nick begged for her forgiveness, but Diana just shouted at him. Would she punish him forever?

It was Diana who broke down in therapy. For her this was a watershed. Nick had not realised just how fragile she was. Her whole world had crashed; she was a wounded little girl. They both had to work through their anger and shame, to do some growing up before they could move on. Sex was way down the line. Nick could not compartmentalise his foolish act, for sex had consequences; Diana needed to feel better about herself and find the generosity to forgive him. After many painful sessions they eventually established enough mutual trust and were able to make love again. To their relief, the sex was tender and healing.

***

David and Chloe had been married for 19 years. Sex had never really been important to either of them, but then David was caught out in such a banal way when Chloe emptied the pockets of his suit and found receipts for a nightclub. When she confronted him he had to admit that he had taken a lap dancer to a hotel room but he had not been able to have sex with her – his erection had failed. That wasn't the point as far as Chloe was concerned. Years of suppressed resentment and anger came to the surface: this was not the man she had fallen in love with, the man she had wanted to build a shared life with. It had all been a sham! He was sneaky and base, she couldn't possibly stay with him.

To David's immense surprise, Chloe left him. One night of foolishness had destroyed his marriage and it wasn't even about sex, it was about his weakness of character. Chloe realised that she had fallen in love with an idealised fantasy, not the real man. It took courage to leave him, but she felt surprisingly liberated and perfectly able to live on her own and relish her independence; she didn't need a sexual partner. David, however, was miserable and lonely on his own. Soon he became involved with another woman because he needed looking after. He never really got his erection back, but she didn't seem to mind.

All three men did something foolish and thought they could compartmentalise their one-night stand as if it didn't really count, but there were inevitable consequences.

Betrayal is always betrayal.

Insights from the therapist

Monogamy is hard work. We live in an age that focuses on the needs of the individual, we have unrealistically high expectations and a desire for instant gratification. How can we be expected to remain faithful to our partner for thirty, forty, maybe fifty years? But look what happened to Bill, Nick and David who somehow thought their flings didn't count.

Moving on from the honeymoon 'in love' phase to the 'loving' phase affects desire. One's high expectations can no longer be met, the loss of excitement is not tolerated and the partner is no longer experienced as a sexual being. 'I don't fancy him/her anymore' and 'the spark has gone' are the two most common complaints I hear. Sex, like most factors in a relationship, needs attention. It's all too easy for it to become routine and boring, and couples need to find ways of making it special again.

The monotony of monogamy can wear us down. We become institutionalised in a semi-happy relationship. We stay together for the kids and the mortgage, the fear of being alone, the safety of the familiar and the habitual, and because it's expected of us. This truly is the post-romantic marriage and it's not very sexy. Tolerance of boredom and loss of energy are inconducive to a fulfilling sex life. We cannot afford to be lazy. Yet monogamy has to be the default position because it embodies faith, trust, stability and moral certainty. The challenge of monogamy is that it's all or nothing. One can't be a little bit monogamous or a little bit unfaithful, and we may have to make sacrifices to achieve monogamy.

A lasting relationship needs to be based on a secure attachment, emotional reciprocity and sexual desire. Sexual desire may be the most fragile element – it needs nurturing. There is a conflict between long-term sexual exclusivity and sexual variety. The hard work of monogamy is that both parties have to believe in it, be proactive, and together take responsibility for their sex life. The alternatives to monogamy are scary: familiarity is safe, affection less dangerous than desire. Yet we want to feel special and admired, to be validated as sexual beings. We need to be reassured that we are still attractive in midlife, we want to be desired, to satisfy the greed of having our cake and eating it. Temptation is everywhere, yet we are asked to want what we already have and not have what we want.

Sex is what makes a monogamous relationship different from friendship, being siblings or flatmates. It's a special and unique bond, and it's also a life-force with its own energy. Our sexuality is a part of us. If we shut it down then we are missing out on something important. The less we do it, the less we want to do it.

Many people in midlife find themselves stuck in sexless marriages and enforced celibacy. This in itself attacks desire, which can just wither and die like a plant in drought. There are challenging solutions that will only work if there is mutual trust and no major under-lying anger or resentment in the relationship.

'Just do it . . .' This might sound pretty spontaneous, but it needs a lot of intimacy and prolonged foreplay to start with. Going from famine to feast is difficult, but giving more attention and affection is a good start. Little physical gestures can build intimacy, like holding hands, a friendly arm round a shoulder, non-sexual hugs, the occasional kiss.

'We agree to make love once a week for at least six months . . .' This sounds good, but just how feasible is it? Though somewhat contrived, it could be fun. The more you do it, the more you want it. However, an agreement of this kind is like a contract, a bit businesslike. Agree on the small print and the get-out clauses before taking it on. Try to make it romantic in some way.

'We will spend a night or a weekend alone together and make love . . .' You both have to be up for this. It requires advance planning and realistic expectations. It's not spontaneous but it could be romantic. Once is not enough, though.

'I can't be bothered . . .', 'I'm too tired/stressed/busy . . .', 'I've lost interest. . .' Cop-out or choice? It's up to you, but there may be a price to pay, as we saw with Steve and Karen and Mark and Kate.

Sexless marriages have led to a huge growth in online dating sites for the purpose of adultery. Advocates say it's actually a way of protecting their marriage by avoiding a full-blown affair and the risk of divorce. They insist it's harmless fun, but is cheating fun? Can you manage the guilt and the fear of being caught out?

Amy's husband had lost interest in sex because he worked 14-hour days and was always exhausted and stressed. Their children were busy teenagers and out a lot. By contrast, Amy had time on her hands and she was bored. Once she started to look at Internet sites, she soon found one for married people. She felt she had nothing to lose and she would be meeting people in similar circumstances. After choosing someone whose photo looked attractive, she started chatting online. They seemed to have enough in common. Very quickly the conversation grew flirty and then quite dirty or 'erotic', as she liked to think. She felt thrilled by this illicit connection.

He offered to take her out to dinner in a hotel restaurant. She was nervous but excited to meet him at last. He was not as good-looking as his photo and quite a bit older, which disappointed her, but she was up for it. Conversation over dinner was a bit stilted but he asked her if she'd go up to his room. She tried to imagine having sex with him and said yes.

The encounter was not exactly wonderful. Foreplay was perfunctory. He put a condom on and thrust into her. It hurt and she gasped. He pumped away and grunted as he came. Rolling off her, he finished her off with his finger. It was efficient but completely soulless. When they left, he said he'd be in touch, but she did not want to see him again; she felt used.

At home Amy thought very carefully about her marriage: her husband was a good man, but it had been a while since they had paid attention to each other. She did not want anonymous sex, she wanted love and intimacy. Tears ran down her face as she thought about what she had done, how she had put her marriage at risk; how destructive her selfish and childish behaviour had been in this tawdry act of mechanical sex with a virtual stranger.

They needed a break, time alone together again. Amy discussed this with her husband and eventually he agreed. She booked a long weekend away and tried to live down her guilt and self-disgust.

Nigel was married but lonely. His wife was visiting relatives in Canada and was away for two whole weeks. But he had been feeling lonely for a long time: the thrill had gone. They'd been half-heartedly trying for a baby but nothing had happened. He hadn't enjoyed the lovemaking, which was supposed to be baby-making. His life stretched out ahead of him and it made him feel anxious. He was bored. So he went online because it was that simple and he found Edie. Edie was an art-lover and rather beautiful. She was in a relationship but described it as 'going nowhere'. This is what he told me:

'We met at a smart gastro pub and talked all night. It was fun and sexually charged. On a whim I said, "I'll take you to Florence for a long weekend." She was up for it.

'We didn't see much art – we spent most of the time

in bed. She was an amazing woman, easy to please, no inhibitions whatsoever, willing to try anything. She knew what the deal was, that I was playing away. When we got back I told her I could not see her again. I had had an amazing adventure, but it was over. It had been exhilarating but it was over. I was staying married – I could never make a commitment to her so it was over. She cried silently as we parted. I felt a twinge of guilt, but no regrets. In fact I was feeling pretty good and determined to make my marriage more interesting and fulfilling.

'I missed the signs. Edie sent me innocuous texts, which I foolishly replied to without encouraging her in any way. Then she started calling me and leaving sexy messages on my voicemail. I did not want this and told her so. She tracked down where I worked and would stand outside at the end of the day, waiting for me. This was beyond a joke. I was getting worried now. I ducked out through the back – I did not want her following me and finding out where I lived. I started to delete all her messages without reading or listening to them.

'Then it got serious. She left a note for me in reception at work, threatening to kill herself. I had to meet her. I didn't know what to do. How unstable was she? Was she really going to kill herself? I realised that I knew her body inside out but I did not know her mind; I knew virtually nothing about her.

'I met her in a Starbucks, bad coffee and unromantic. Edie looked haunted. She told me she loved me and wept. I told her I did not love her and was firm. She said she would kill herself and I half-believed her. I had to do something to get us both out of this dangerous situation. What would I do for someone I really cared about? Then it came to me: I made her call her GP and make an emergency appointment. She was in a daze but she obeyed me. I took her there and went in with her. I told the GP the entire story such as it was and said that I could not be responsible for a depressed stalker. Then I walked out, leaving her there. It was a shitty thing to do and I wasn't proud of myself.

'Luckily for me I never heard from Edie again but I didn't feel good about it. I thought I'd better make a real effort with my wife, maybe take her away somewhere – it certainly would not be Florence!'

Both Amy and Nigel had got away with their online dating affairs but they had been bruised. Extramarital dating is not for the faint-hearted – it's about being bold and adventurous, with a clear understanding of what one is getting into. Usually there is little emotional involvement or intimacy in these sexual encounters. Don't expect a romantic courtship; you're expected to get right down to business, as Amy discovered. In a consumer society this is more about satisfying hunger with a fix of fast food. For Nigel it was about the thrill of danger and risk, but there could have been a heavy price to pay.

People fantasise about webcam sex and no-strings sex sites. They are looking for casual sex and porn-style sex with no commitment and they think they are in control. And what about the further shores of sex? Some are attracted to open relationships, wife swapping, swinging, threesomes, group sex, BDSM clubs. Putting this kind of sexual behaviour into action crosses a frontier.

Fuzzy boundaries are difficult to manage and generally suit one partner more than the other. Sex becomes voyeuristic and perverse with little emotional attachment or real intimacy. Usually there are issues of power and control. A recent example of this is the behaviour of former chief of the IMF Dominique Strauss-Kahn with the hotel chambermaid, prostitutes and orgies. His rising star in international finance and politics crashed to earth.

One partner may go along with extreme behaviour in order to keep the relationship going. Jealousy looms large because most people do not wish to share themselves or their partner with anyone else, however free-thinking they appear to be. Sex becomes desensitised and the search for pleasure more compulsive. This is the danger when acting out sexual fantasies that go beyond the usual boundaries of an exclusive relationship.

Faithfulness, trust and intimacy are the bedrock of a long-term committed sexual relationship but they cannot be taken for granted.

CHAPTER FOUR

Sex, Love and Porn Addiction

Internet porn

Henry was a senior executive in a multinational corporation who travelled abroad a lot. He had lived in New York, Hong Kong and Singapore. At first he seemed to be a cheerful and gregarious person, but he had a haggard, driven look about him, almost furtive – a darker side. His wife Jeanne was from a French bourgeois Catholic family. She looked miserable and tense. There was something grim about this couple.

It turned out that they had both been treated for depression on and off for several years, but nevertheless they put on a bright face. Henry had gone through a massive burnout at work and had had to take four months' sick leave. During this time Jeanne had become his carer and had put up with his black moods and irrational insults. She did everything for him; he needed her to organise his life and look after him. During that time he had been angry and abusive with her. To me Henry seemed very discontented with the life he was leading but he was a workaholic who could never say no, an overachiever who never felt good enough. Despite the stress, he eventually chose to escape back to work because the familiar routine gave his daily life some kind of meaningful structure. Still pretty fragile emotionally, he was very much in danger of crashing again.

Henry had taken huge risks at work, accessing hard porn sites several times a day on his computer in a fairly open-plan office. Did any of his colleagues know? Probably, but then some of them must have been doing it too. It was just a game. A dangerous and illicit game that made it even more thrilling. He used to masturbate at his desk when he could, or in the toilets.

Henry did not see how sordid his behaviour was, for the compulsive nature of his addiction had gripped him. He also needed mothering. His own mother had been overprotective and had spoilt him. His father had left when he was four and he had always been jealous of his brothers. His mother quickly remarried and he hated his stepfather. Henry knew nothing about sex in his early adolescence, but he masturbated a lot with *Playboy* magazines. He had always suffered from premature ejaculation and was never bothered about giving the few women he slept with any pleasure – paying for it was easier.

Sex with Jeanne was out of the question now: he had lost all desire for her long ago and she was frozen. He had ended up marrying a woman who did not really enjoy sex, which let him off the hook. Sex had always been a bit of an obligation for Jeanne and she had never wanted to explore her sexuality; she was too uptight and repressed. In any case Henry blamed his loss of desire on her four pregnancies and the way her body had changed. Although she had more or less got her figure back each time, Jeanne took the blame: she felt she disgusted him.

For Henry cruising porn sites on the Internet had been a revelation. Here was the gateway to all those forbidden fantasies – big breasts and shaven women, anal and oral sex, dominatrix in leather and chains, women tied up and whipped, girl on girl, threesomes, violent orgies . . . It was an escape into another world and all he had to do was pay and watch, no engagement, no commitment, no responsibility. Here was instant satisfaction and he was in control of it. Except that he wasn't – the insidious power of the Internet and the ubiquity of porn had taken control of him. The hit to the brain was the same as any substance abuse. You can abstain from alcohol and drugs, you can abstain from sex, but in the modern world, how could he give up the computer?

Jeanne finally addressed the elephant in the room and blurted out the major problem: Henry was addicted to Internet porn and had been watching it on the computer for at least ten years. He had also been using sex chat-lines. At first he had said it was just a bit of naughty fun, which upset her. She was naïve and confused, but later, when she found out what he was really watching, she felt not just betrayed and humiliated but profoundly shocked and disgusted. Henry kept telling her that it was all in the past, but she knew he was lying. He was in complete denial and would not acknowledge that he had a problem. Pure addict-speak.

Jeanne suspected that he had recently been using prostitutes, and she challenged him. He said it wasn't true but she shouldn't make it a self-fulfilling prophecy (thus transferring his guilt onto her). Almost certainly he was still accessing porn and lying about it.

Jeanne could not find the courage to leave him – there was too much at stake for her, she was not strong enough to be on her own. She felt helpless and hopeless. Here was the classic codependent partner of an addict, sweeping the dirt under the carpet, switching back and forth from the controller/rescuer role and the martyr/victim role, but the fixed smile on her face was fast turning into a grimace.

There was little doubt nothing had been resolved during Henry's time off work and he was at serious risk of another breakdown. Anxious and panicky, he was always turning angrily on her. She in turn was lonely and despairing. Both were in a highly unstable psychological state.

Henry was vulnerable and increasingly depressed. He admitted to suicidal thoughts and confessed that he had been hoarding his medication. Was he suicidal? He needed to be in treatment in a safe place, but first he had to admit to being an addict and to say that he wanted to save his marriage and his career. Following this he had to agree to go into rehab, probably for four to six weeks, where he would follow the Twelve-Step Recovery Program for addiction.

The Twelve-Step Program is tough. Lies, deception and excuses are challenged by the peer group, and the addict will not get away with bullshitting or feeling sorry for himself. However awful his personal story, it will always be matched by someone else's. He will discover that honesty is the only way forward and he will start to take responsibility for himself and stop blaming others. It's hard and requires commitment and motivation. Knowing one is not alone is immensely supportive. There is also the relief of being with others who share the same unbearable feelings, such as shame, guilt, self-destructiveness and anxiety. In rehab, being accepted and understood by a nonjudgemental therap-ist brings healing. Insight, awareness and a willingness to make permanent changes will help recovery, but once an addict, always an addict – there is no cure. On leaving rehab the addict will need to attend Twelve-Step meetings in order to maintain recovery. At first it is one day at a time: 'Today, I choose not to . . .' Some people become dependent on the meetings, but that is less harmful than their habit.

Partners need support too. Jeanne had to learn to be independent, not codependent. She too had to take responsibility for herself and not blame Henry for everything. She had to stop enabling him, stop bending over backwards in order to meet his perceived needs;

she needed to find her own voice, express her own fears and anger. Only then could she find forgiveness. Their entire relationship had to be renegotiated.

This truly was a massive midlife crisis that would take a long time to resolve. Only then was there a chance of healing the marriage and starting their sexual relationship again from scratch. The odds were long. I was not optimistic when it came to their chances, because after Henry's stay in rehab, I did not hear from them again.

Can't get enough

Though a good-looking man in his mid-thirties, Cliff had a haunted look and tense body language. There was something almost creepy in the way he held my gaze, a false intimacy that felt imposed on me, but I listened carefully to his story.

'I live with my partner Marilyn but actually we don't have sex very often. She's a bit of a cold one, but I feel safe with her, no surprises. She never asks me where I am or what I'm up to. Just as well, because I keep pretty busy.

'I try to see my friend Shirley every couple of weeks. I've known her all my life – she's older than me, married. I confide in her, she never judges me. Sex with her is comforting; she's my fuck buddy. Then there's Cheryl. Cheryl is my sex slave – she'll do anything for me. I can dress her up in rubber, tie her down, blindfold her, fuck her any which way. Sometimes we do three-somes, two girls and me, or another bloke – that turns me on. I also like to have sex with Cheryl in public places, it's a real thrill.' He looked at me defiantly, but I held steady.

'I work in a shoe shop, I'm the manager – I meet a lot of women, I'm good with the chat. When I strike lucky, we have quick sex in the back of the storeroom. I've never been caught, it's exciting doing it like that – I'd get the sack if anyone found out.'

This was a man who was living dangerously, end-lessly seeking pleasure, but I could tell how grim the reality was, how profoundly desperate and unhappy he was.

'Then there's Jilly. Jilly is my beautiful angel. She works on reception at my doctors' surgery. I've fallen in love with her, but she won't have it. It's driving me nuts – I've tried everything but there's nothing doing. It makes me feel wretched. Then I have to have sex or I get really panicky.'

Sex was the only way Cliff could manage his anx-iety. He told me later that when he gets desperate he cruises the streets in his car and picks up a prostitute. If he doesn't have time to do that, he watches hard porn online and masturbates. His life is one long search for sex and more sex. That is sex addiction. It's not glamorous or fun, but compulsive and driven – a way of warding off feelings of fear and shame, depression and the inner emptiness of one's existence.

What caused Cliff's sex addiction? The answer partly lay in his childhood experiences. He was the oldest of five children and his mother was a bipolar psychotic (violent mood swings, suicide attempts and crazed manic behaviour); she was in and out of psychiatric hospitals. His father was an overworked farmer who couldn't cope with the children. When Cliff was seven, he and his siblings were taken into care, at which point he was sexually abused by several carers. He worried constantly that it would make him gay so he started having sex with girls in the home when he was fifteen. From the age of sixteen he had to fend for himself out in the world.

Cliff was an emotional orphan. He missed his mother whom he hardly knew, and the mothering he had never had; sex seemed to be the answer. At first it made him feel really good about himself and helped him cope with his anxiety and depression, but over the years his constant need for sex with different people took hold and he just couldn't get enough of it. Now he was caught in the spiral of addiction.

Although I was at least twenty years older than Cliff, he tried to be seductive with me. He tested me over and over. Would I go out to dinner with him? Could he take me to one of his private clubs? Would I have sex with him, he'd make it really good? No, no and no! He seemed almost relieved that he couldn't have me and that's when the deeper work started. Cliff gradually understood that his behaviour was not only self-destructive but also fed by an unconscious need to punish those who had let him down. 'Find 'em, fuck 'em, forget 'em' was his revenge. Consumed with guilt and shame that added to his sense of worthlessness, he became very depressed and I was concerned for him. Eventually he accepted that the only path to healing and reparation lay in abstention, but he dreaded the panic attacks. I taught him some basic breathing techniques and some mindful relaxation as a substitute for sexual activity to take him through the panic attacks. He took some convincing, but it worked in emergencies. Cliff was beginning to go through the unbearable feelings that had haunted him for so long and come out the other side, fragile and shaky.

I told Cliff that his only hope of full recovery lay in being totally celibate for the time being, however frightening that might feel. He needed to get up every morning and say, 'Today, I choose not to have sex', one day at a time. Only then would he be able to face his fears and overcome his feelings. Then maybe he would eventually be able to come through the despair and fear to form a truly meaningful, close and loving relationship with just one woman. It would be a long and painful journey.

Cliff managed to give up all his sexual partners and later told me, 'I really didn't think I could do it – it was a massive change. I know I will always be at risk but now I understand my behaviour was not really about sex, it was about the fear of unbearable feelings.'

Addicted to love

'I've never been without a man in my life . . .' A handsome woman in her mid-forties, Jessica was divorced with a teenage son. She went on: 'I grew up with two older brothers who spoiled me. Mum was a bit of a doormat, Dad was very dashing – *too* dashing, it turned out. He had a long-term mistress and probably some girlfriends on the side, but it was never talked about. My marriage went wrong after a couple of years because my husband found out I was unfaithful. It wasn't serious but he was the jealous type – I did it because I was bored. I have had several lovers since my divorce but none of them was prepared to make a commitment so I kept moving on.' Jessica talked as though she was in control of her relationships but now she was very upset.

'I met Sam at a party – there was instant chemistry, we could barely keep our hands off each other. He was there with his wife, a forlorn little woman, but that didn't put me off. We managed to meet up two or three times a week and I was having fantastic hot sex every time – it was amazing, I couldn't get enough of it. He told me his divorce was coming through. We were head over heels in love. He didn't want to live in my house, he wanted us to buy a house of our own as soon as he was free of his financial obligations (he ran his own business and money didn't seem to be a problem).

'We had an idyllic holiday later that year and then we started house hunting. I put my house on the market.

It took a while but eventually we found a lovely house, although it did need some work. I had an architect friend who agreed to help – he was one of my exes but there was no point in telling Sam. I had a reasonable offer on my house, we were just waiting to exchange on ours.

'One day I dropped by his office to surprise him and maybe take him out for the afternoon. I was flushed with desire, imagining how we would make love. His ex-wife was there, which I hadn't expected, and she seemed to be arguing with Debbie, the receptionist. The atmosphere was pretty heated. She took one look at me and said, "Who are you? I expect you're one more in the chain!" Confused, I thought she was talking about property exchanges.

'"You do realise he's having an affair with her?" she said, pointing to Debbie, who looked extremely uncomfortable. "What about the divorce?" I blurted out. "*Divorce!* What divorce? Is that what he told you? We're not getting divorced!' she shouted. I left. I couldn't believe what I had just heard – we were in love, he was the love of my life.

'When I confronted Sam later that day, he calmed me down.

'"Darling, take no notice of her, she's mad, completely delusional. This is the sort of thing she does all the time. I love you and very soon we'll be together in our new house," he told me. We made love; I gave it my all.

'Time went by and there were endless delays in exchanging contracts. I called him at work. It was time to have a chat with Debbie.

'"Hi, it's Jessica," I said, "I just want to ask you a couple of things."

'"Oh, yes," she replied. "Jessica, I think you should know that Sam and I have just got engaged. We're going to get married next year, after I've had the baby. I'm pregnant, you see. I'm so happy!"

'I felt sick – what was going on? Was I going mad? I felt like I'd been punched in the stomach. When I asked Sam for an explanation he confessed to having had a one-night fling with Debbie, actually not even a night, and most unfortunately she had fallen pregnant. And yes, of course he was getting divorced, he really loved me and wanted to be with me and could I forgive him for the "slip"?

'I told him I never wanted to see him again – I just couldn't believe that this wonderful man had behaved so badly. And I was so in love with him, but who was he? Did I really know him? The sexual chemistry had blinded me; I had wanted him so badly.

'He turned up on my doorstep with flowers and champagne and the most beautiful bracelet. He touched my arm and I crumpled, overwhelmed with desire. We didn't make it as far as the bedroom, we had sex on the floor, half-undressed, and then we went to bed for the rest of the day and made love for hours. He left the next morning without a word.

'He tried so hard to get me back, wooing me with more flowers and presents, begging me for forgiveness. I gave in every time because I missed him so dreadfully. I wanted to feel his body next to mine, hot and hard, taking me rhythmically to the heights of passion and desire until we both exploded into orgasm. This couldn't go on, it would destroy me. I didn't know what to believe, what to do; who to turn to. He was messing with my mind, making me think I was crazy. Crazy in love, yes!

'He promised me I was his only love but I could not believe him anymore. Then I did something I was dreading, but there was no other way: I hired a private detective. I received his report after a couple of weeks – Sam was still living at home with his wife, no divorce had been filed. Debbie had had her baby and was on maternity leave. He visited her regularly, loaded with flowers and shopping bags. Worst of all was the information that Sam used an escort service and regularly met with call girls at hotels. I felt dirty and contaminated and shuddered at the thought of the risks I had taken with unprotected sex. He was a sex addict and a compulsive liar. And I was a codependent love-addict who had tacitly agreed to his destructive behaviour in order to meet my own needs for affirmation.'

Understanding the nature of addiction and how it had affected Jessica as a willing partner was the beginning of her work in therapy. After several months of painful self-discovery, she understood that she had to be on her own and take responsibility for herself.

Jessica says in conclusion: 'Finally I realised I had to learn to be alone and be responsible for myself – I couldn't allow myself to be used and hurt again. I was really scared but I had to face my own demons and be alone and celibate without feeling lonely and unloved. It was very hard but I couldn't go through that kind of devastating pain again.'

Insights from the therapist

Is there really such a thing as sex addiction? After all, sex is not a substance like alcohol or heroin. Isn't it just an excuse for faithless footballers and spoilt celebs to have sex whenever they feel like it? Does it justify the tabloid headlines and rehab fees?

If someone is using compulsive sex as an escape from unbearable feelings and becomes anxious and panicky without frequent sexual activity, then one can start to think of her or his behaviour in terms of addiction. Sex addicts, like most other addicts, are trying to fill the emptiness inside, the black hole of depression, fear, anxiety and shame. Sexual bulimia is a repetitive pattern of sexual binge and guilt with a desperate search for comfort and relief. Addiction is not a question of weakness or willpower, it's a complex psychological and physical condition driven by dependence and compulsion. One can become addicted to an activity like gambling or sex. They too pump up the adrenalin and access the pleasure centres in the brain. Addiction is mood altering, it's anaesthetising; it's an escape from unbearable feelings. It takes one from reward to relief. But what once gave pleasure and enjoyment becomes something one has to have more and more of in order to function without constant feelings of anxiety or panic. Craving often goes along with denial and a false belief that one is in control. The addict's behaviour becomes compulsive and destructive – relationships are harmed, lives ruined.

The drug of sex is no longer recreational. Need becomes obsessive, enough is never enough.

Very often men who need non-stop sex have had cold, unloving mothers who have rejected or abandoned them, as in Cliff's case. Here, the unconscious hope is of somehow finding through repeated sexual connection the missing emotional connection to the unavailable or absent mother. The power of the penis may also be a way of persecuting and punishing the bad mother and women in general. It's not about pleasure and fun or even notches on the bedpost.

Another example is Hugh Hefner, the founder of Playboy magazine and a hugely successful sex industry. Now in his eighties, he is never without two or three busty young blondes by his side and in his bed. Hefner once said in an interview that he did not have a single memory of being hugged or touched by his mother. I believe he has turned to an endless supply of sexually available young women to make up for the lack of maternal affection.

Hollywood legend Marilyn Monroe, who lived and breathed sex, never knew her father. Her schizophrenic mother was hospitalised during her childhood and she was fostered, sexually abused and placed in an orphanage. At sixteen she married her first husband. Marilyn called Arthur Miller, her third husband, 'Daddy'. She wanted to be taken seriously as an actress but she is remembered for being a sexual icon who used her fabulous body in an increasingly desperate search for love.

Women with a compulsive need for sex are generally using their bodies as a way of ensuring their emotional needs are met. In the search for attention and affection they also hope that sex will bring them attachment and intimacy. They want approval and reassurance, but their behaviour gets them nowhere and they can become increasingly neurotic and manipulative. Used and abused, they are frequently rejected by their sexual partners, who are unwilling or unable to give them what they really need. This increases their sense of worthlessness, which feeds their destructive behaviour and sexual acting out. These women are frequently the daughters of distant or unavailable fathers, who have never been validated by a safe man as attractive young women. Looking for comfort and affirmation through sex, they become addicted to love.

The way to overcome any addiction is to go back to the causes. This means exploring family patterns in childhood that may have caused deep feelings of fear and anxiety. If there has not been enough good parenting, often the child will grow up feeling worthless and undeserving. This may lead to self-destructive behaviour, thus proving one is unlovable. Add guilt, shame and possibly a genetic disposition to the mix and it is only too easy to turn to substance abuse or addictive behaviour. The key to recovery is abstinence, learning how to manage the unbearable feelings and rebuilding self-esteem. It's hard work that requires a real commitment.

CHAPTER FIVE

Sexual Abuse

Shameful secrets

Suzy was a pretty young woman with long, fair hair and china-blue eyes. But Suzy was fat, *very* fat. What was her obesity concealing, I wondered. She sat down heavily and started straight in.

'Yes, I'm fat,' she announced cheerfully, although she looked anything but cheerful, 'Mummy stuffed me with cakes and biscuits and sweeties when I was little for being a good girl. Then after Daddy left,' she paused, holding back the tears, her voice faltering, 'she was so horrible to me. I used to buy cakes with my pocket money and hide them in my room. I'd eat them at night. Then she told me that no one would ever love me because I was so fat and ugly so I used to make myself sick.'

These were the classic symptoms of bulimia. We needed to work towards the 'why', not the 'what' and 'how'. Over several sessions Suzy and I talked about her eating disorder. She was still bingeing and she felt so ashamed; she was desperate for comfort and food was where she found it. Her mother had used food to control her, both as a punishment and as a reward. Suzy had been conditioned.

Like many addictive substances, food (literally) fills the emptiness within, the black hole of despair. Our relationship with eating can be so complex. We need to eat to survive so we can't give it up entirely, unlike drugs or alcohol. Sugary food tastes so good and gives us a glucose rush. No wonder we love cakes and biscuits, and of course, anything to do with chocolate. The pounds pile on and we start to hate our bodies. Some people find the feelings of guilt and shame intolerable. Making themselves sick is a way of taking control, but the underlying feelings of worthlessness and the loss of self-esteem cannot be vomited away so the vicious cycle of bingeing starts up again.

Suzy would talk non-stop in her sessions, purging herself of unbearable feelings, rather like making herself sick. Did she leave and immediately gorge herself? Was I not 'feeding' her well enough? It would take time. We focused a lot on her difficult relationship with her mother, who was not only cold and unloving but, I suspected, jealous of her daughter's good looks. At the same time I knew there was something else going on in Suzy's mind, but we hadn't quite got there yet.

One day Suzy came in, sat down and slumped in her chair, gazing at me in silence. I felt unusually nervous and apprehensive, which obviously reflected her feelings. As I waited for her to speak, the silence grew heavier. Now Suzy was avoiding eye contact, hiding behind her long hair. I wanted to break the silence but I knew I mustn't: something important was coming.

'Daddy . . .' she said at last in a small, little girl's voice. It was the first time she had ever mentioned him; this could be a breakthrough. I said nothing. 'Daddy used to read to me at night. Then he started getting into the bed "so that we can cuddle". Mummy never hugged me so I loved that – he would tickle me very gently and make me giggle. Then he started visiting me in the night because he'd had a bad dream or he couldn't sleep and he said tickling would help him. He started tickling me down there, between my legs. It made me squirm but I liked it. Then I had to tickle his willy – it got so big! Then we played rubbing games; I still liked it. He told how much he loved me and how pretty I was, and that we had this special private tickling secret. One night he told me his willy wanted to go inside me. He put cream on it and pushed it into me, with his hand on my mouth so I wouldn't make a noise. It hurt. I was a bit scared and didn't like this game at all. He'd give me chocolates afterwards.

'One night he badly hurt me – he made me really sore and bleeding. I didn't want to upset him so in the morning I told Mummy. She was so angry, her face went quite white: "I knew he was up to something, the dirty bastard! Right, that's it!" she said. Mummy packed me off to school. That night I heard lots of shouting and clattering and doors slamming. Daddy didn't come to my room, but I wanted him to. I didn't understand what was happening, I was scared.

'Daddy loved me, I know he did, but he left because of me, Mummy says. I came down to breakfast and said, "Where's Daddy?" "Gone!" she screamed, "because of you and your wicked lies!" I felt cold and frightened. I never saw him again and he was never mentioned again, ever. Why didn't he come for me? I had told our private secret; it was all my fault. I was only six . . .' She paused, with a bewildered hurt look on her face, like the little six-year-old girl she once was.

'After that I became a very quiet and obedient child. Mummy was very cold with me. I kept my head down and worked hard at school because the teachers liked me. The other children called me names because I was fat, but I didn't care. Eating sweet things made me feel better and I was careful always to have biscuits and sweets with me wherever I went.'

When Suzy had finished her account of this abuse she gave me a wild look and fled from the room. Throughout the session I hadn't said a word. I feared she would now stuff herself with cakes and pastries to submerge her overwhelming feelings of guilt and shame; she had 'vomited' all over me.

As I expected, Suzy missed our next session. It had been too painful, talking about her terrible secret. I was concerned – did she trust me enough to resume the therapy? The following week she returned, looking a little shy but much calmer and somehow more adult.

'You are the only person I have told about what my father did. I loved him so much I wanted to please him. I wanted him to touch me even though it was wrong and he hurt me. I am still so confused, I still miss him,' she told me.

We talked a lot about her father, not just the sexual abuse but also about his sudden departure and how Suzy felt responsible for him leaving because she had betrayed him. He had not contacted her since, which upset her, but part of her was also relieved.

Incest has dreadful consequences. In every society it is taboo for good reasons, and when that taboo is broken it affects the whole family. The biggest loss is that of innocence, of childhood, and the loss of parents as good-enough father and mother, whose duties are to love, cherish and protect their children from harm. Mothers are usually in denial; victims are often accused of lying because the truth is too terrible.

For reasons of her own, the mother may be unable to maintain a healthy sexual relationship with her partner and therefore at some deep unconscious level it may actually suit her for the daughter or son to take on her sexual role. At least it keeps it in the family. The scenario is complicated if the mother has hidden feelings of envy, jealousy and rivalry. In any case the victim is effectively let down and abandoned by the one person he/she would normally turn to for help, on top of all the complications in the relationship with the father. He too is lost to him/her once the secret is revealed.

A few weeks later Suzy told me in her little-girl voice that she had another secret. Again there was the long silence, the lack of eye contact. I knew not to speak. What was she going to tell me? I genuinely had no idea but I prepared myself for something terrible.

'I was drunk the first time I had sex. I didn't feel anything one way or the other but I did like the hugging – it made me feel like a little girl again. So that was my sex life, nothing to get excited about and only with men who liked big women, which wasn't many. My friend Carrie says I'm curvy, not fat, but I still can't bear to look in the mirror. And if I disgust myself, how can anyone else bear to look at me?' There followed a long, sad silence.

'One evening Stan from work rang my doorbell. I was surprised – I didn't think he was interested in me. He looked nice in his tight jeans and leather jacket, a real cool operator. He grinned at me, which made me squirm. I don't know why, it just did.

'"Come on," he said, "let's grab a curry and go to the Paradise Lounge."

'I think I blushed. He'd chosen *me* to go to this club place! I don't like curry and I can't dance, but he'd chosen *me*! I was so excited, my head was spinning.

'Anyway, in the restaurant I managed to get some of the curry down and pushed the rest around the plate. Mummy wouldn't have approved, but Mummy wasn't there. She made me sit at the table, sometimes for hours, until I'd eaten everything on the plate. I'd be crying and gagging and retching, but she just used to laugh.

'So then we get to the Paradise Lounge. It was hot, noisy and crowded. Stan kept giving me these pink drinks – vodka, I think it was. He took all my cash from my purse to pay the bill.

'I don't remember much after that. I felt all strange and woozy; Stan kissed me a lot. I liked that. Next thing I know, I wake up in the dark and things are not right. I must be in his flat. There's this crushing weight on top of me, grunting. He's ramming into me. I'm all pain and I can't breathe; I try to scream but it comes out as a moan and he says, "Like it, do you, you fat slag?"'

Suzy's voice had gone quieter and quieter. I wanted to lean forward towards her but I didn't want to scare her.

'He rolls off me, my thighs are sticky and I sort of choke. I know I'm going to throw up so I look for the bathroom and end up being sick in the kitchen sink – must've been the curry,' she continued. 'He throws my clothes at me and shouts, "Get out!" I didn't know what to do – I was shaking and crying. He goes into the bedroom, shuts the door and I'm standing there alone, half-naked, raped.

'Yeah, raped. There, I've said it out loud: I was raped, that's what it was, rape.'

Suzy went silent again, reliving the dazed state she had been in. 'Yes, you were raped,' I said, wanting her to hear me confirm it. She continued her story of that dreadful night.

'Out in the street I didn't know where I was – I had to look at the map at a bus stop. There were no buses at that time, of course. I walked for about an hour. It was all quiet, not a light on anywhere, darkness all around me. I was so scared, I tried to sing a few lines from The Beatles' "Yellow Submarine" like I used to with Daddy, but I had lost my voice and Daddy wasn't there.'

Tears rolled down her face. She truly was an emotional orphan – I wanted to give her a big, motherly hug, but of course I couldn't.

'All I ever wanted was to feel safe,' she went on. 'I thought Stan would hug me and hold me and make me feel safe. I thought he might care, but they don't, do they? I feel like a dirty piece of rubbish – that's all I am really, rubbish. I had to tell someone but I couldn't, I was so ashamed. At work I just kept my head down and avoided Stan. I could tell Daddy – he'd listen, he'd understand . . . But Daddy was gone. So now I've told you.'

Suzy was sobbing quietly. I passed her the tissues. 'Thank you for telling me,' I said, feeling a deep respect for her – it had taken so much courage to reveal her secret. 'I appreciate how hard it is to talk about the terrible things that have happened to you.'

'I never want to have sex with a man again,' she added in a miserable voice.

Her experiences had been so traumatic; I could understand that.

So how did Suzy find healing? Here was her final secret, which came out some weeks later. She came to the session wearing lipstick and she had had her hair cut; she looked confident and cheerful. Looking me straight in the eye, she launched into her story. She was transformed.

'I met Liz at work – Liz was fat, like me, but she seemed quite happy about it. We became friends. Three days ago, after she had cooked a lovely supper for me at her place and we had watched a romantic DVD, she suggested I sleep over because it was so late. She asked if I minded sharing her bed. I told her that was fine.

'Liz held me and touched me and caressed me; she stroked and kissed me. She was very gentle – I'd never had that before. She opened up a world of pleasure I thought I'd never know. It was like coming home. I had found my lover, the love of my life.'

Suzy looked at me with her big blue eyes and gave me a huge warm smile.

She had found her true sexuality.

Teacher's pet

Boys can be victims of abuse too. Here is Steve's story, as told to me.

'I have been carrying a horrible secret all my life. One of my teachers befriended me when I was nine. My dad had left home and I missed him. I was lonely, and this man made me feel special. He told my mum I needed extra lessons. She thought he was doing me a favour – I was a quiet, shy boy with not many friends, a bit lonely.

'We talked a lot about so many interesting things, not just school subjects. He gave me tea and biscuits; he even asked me which ones I liked best. I admired him and I felt flattered. Sometimes we'd go for a walk. He'd put his arm round me, touch my face or hold my hand. One day he showed me his penis and asked me to stroke it. I was too scared to say no. Then the next time he asked me to kiss it. I knew it was wrong but it was also a bit exciting. Afterwards he seemed so grateful.

'A few weeks later, it got worse. He told me to pull down my pants and lean over the table. I was terrified but I couldn't say no. He put some hand cream on his penis and entered me from behind. It hurt the first few times and it really disgusted me, but after a while I got used to it and I'm ashamed to say sometimes I enjoyed it.

'He left the school when I was twelve. It was only a few years later when I started being interested in girls that I realised how wrong it was. But I couldn't tell my mum, I couldn't tell my sister – I was too ashamed. I couldn't tell anyone, it was a dirty secret. I felt very anxious and confused about my body and any physical contact; I didn't want anyone to touch me. At the same time I had strong sexual longings; I was masturbating a lot. I went to the gym all the time and I became a bit bulimic and obsessed about my body and my weight.

'Sometimes I wonder if I'm gay but I don't think I am. I find it very hard being in a relationship. I can't get really intimate and close to anyone – I just don't trust them, I don't feel safe. Sex? I can take it or leave it, I feel a bit anaesthetised.'

Unfortunately this sad story is typical of how a sexual predator grooms and seduces his victim. Children cannot give informed consent to a sexual act and the adult uses his abusive power to terrible effect. Steve and I talked about his story in some detail through many difficult sessions. As he found some relief, he gained in confidence but he still felt safer on his own. But he couldn't get really intimate with me – maybe he just couldn't allow himself to trust me and reveal all his secrets.

The therapy would stop and start, which was symptomatic of his ambivalence. I let him know that I would always wait for him so that he could learn to trust me. Unfortunately victims of abuse are often scarred for life. The best they can hope for is to feel they are not victims but survivors. This is where Steve got to after a year in therapy.

Healing could take a lifetime.

Daddy's girl

Denise and Larry had been married for over twenty years. She had married young to get away from home. Denise was ambivalent about staying in the relationship, although Larry was the only consistent and safe person in her life. She had had several affairs, which he had tolerated. Although he was caring and nurturing, she saw him as weak and needy. The way they interacted in their relationship was codependent and collusive: she taunted and provoked him but he was always there for her.

Denise was an only child and her mother had gone back to work when she was five. Her father had sexually abused her until puberty. She felt abandoned by her mother and his attention made her feel special. After puberty she started giving sexual favours to the older boys at school. She missed her father, who had become a somewhat remote figure, yet she knew what they had shared was wrong. Although she still loved him, she was confused.

When Denise was twenty her father, who was a swimming instructor, was arrested for abusing one of the children in his class. He pleaded guilty and went to prison for three years. Her mother, as usual, refused to talk about it. Denise was very upset, not just because he was going to prison but also because she thought she was the only one; he had been unfaithful to her. Her feelings were split between disgust, anger, guilt and a loving desire to protect him.

When Denise and Larry came to see me, her father was ill with terminal cancer. At this point her relationship with him was distant and polite. She had not forgiven him the abuse or the betrayal. Her promiscuity was as much an attack against him as it was a defence against intimacy with Larry. She was extremely angry with him and she was taking it out on Larry.

Larry had been ill recently, which reminded her of her sexual encounters with her father. She referred to him as 'lying in an unmade bed with used tissues, all messy and sweaty and looking needy'. Denise did not want sex with him in the bedroom – she wanted to do it in settings that were novel and exciting, so that it felt like an affair. Her father came to her bedroom during her childhood. In her inner world her father was her first partner, the love of her life. Her bedroom belonged to him.

Denise went to visit her father after a long gap. He died soon afterwards. She felt angry and guilty but also relieved. Her murderous feelings were still directed at Larry for a while, but at the same time she felt a strong sexual energy towards him. She stopped flirting with other men and started owning the losses that she had undergone by being in an incestuous and abusive relationship. Slowly she moved towards a deeper and more intimate commitment to the marriage and was able to acknowledge Larry's enduring love for her. He had had the patience of a saint because he saw who Denise could be when she was finally free of her father.

Working with Denise, who dominated the therapy, I often felt de-skilled, challenged and not quite good enough. I did not always feel in control. It was difficult knowing what was real and what was fantasy. This reflected Larry's feelings in the marriage. At times all three of us felt confused, and I had to hang on to my professional role and help them untangle the lies and the reality, the doubts and fears, the anger and the ambivalence.

Although Denise and Larry eventually reached some kind of accommodation in their marriage, it was clear that Denise's father had been the love of her life and always would be. Larry just had to accept it for he knew that Denise needed him. This kind of incestuous abuse, with its powerful feelings of love and hate, can be hard to move away from.

Insights from the therapist

My heart sinks when I first hear stories of sexual abuse because there is no easy way through. Speaking honestly and openly about it can be very hard. Are the memories real? What is true and what is fantasy? Hearing about abuse can cause feelings of helplessness or revulsion; one can be curious or judgemental, full of pity or outrage. It is a murky and tricky subject to deal with and one that can arouse very primitive anxieties and often lead to confused thinking. As a therapist one has to keep a clear head and not jump to conclusions. Victims often protect themselves from their trauma by denial or repression, but the therapist must never be intrusive or suggest that they could have been abused. Talking about it is risky for the victim, who may be put back in touch with the overwhelmingly painful and shameful feelings. They may be flooded with sensory memories and relive the original trauma. We have to tread very gently or we can be perceived as abusive ourselves. Both client and therapist are in dangerous territory.

Adult survivors of childhood abuse often display the symptoms of unresolved post-traumatic stress, with nightmares and flashbacks, mood swings and outbursts. They may suffer serious problems such as depression and eating disorders, addiction and self-harm, and may even make suicide attempts. In relationships they may behave in an over-seductive or provocative way. They may be angry or aggressive, or needy, over-involved and over-accommodating. Often they suffer a fear of intimacy and have difficulties with attachment. They will find it hard to allow themselves to be open, vulnerable and trusting – the very attributes needed for good sex. Often they feel conflicted and confused; they are lonely.

Obviously all of this will have an effect on their sex life, which is likely to bring up complex feelings. Survivors of sexual abuse may avoid sex because they have been used and manipulated in situations where they have had no control. Sex is experienced as threatening and unsafe. Sexual abandonment entails trust and vulnerability. It may feel safer to shut down one's desire than to risk the dangers of sex and the temporary loss of self: it's too scary.

Sexual problems are common in victims of childhood sexual abuse, and these include loss of desire, pain, the inability to have penetrative sex or orgasms, and erectile dysfunction in men. These difficulties are all about avoiding sex. Sexual healing is hard and usually requires a lot of therapeutic work, often over several years.

Boys are victims of abuse too. The abuser may be a relative or an authority figure such as a priest or a teacher, and the long-term effects can be devastating. An individual may grow up with lifelong feelings of guilt and shame, low self-esteem and a sense of being defiled. He may have a fear of being gay; he is also likely to have problems with commitment and intimacy and to be anxious about sex.

CHAPTER SIX

Variations

Tie me up, tie me down

Mary had been going out with Bill for several weeks and things were going well. Their sexual relationship was good, if a little intense, and she felt they had a future together. He asked her to spend a weekend with him at his home and she was pleased to accept.

Bill lived in a modern apartment block. His flat was carefully furnished and impeccably tidy. When Mary arrived on the Friday evening he took her straight to the kitchen bar and mixed her a cocktail. Then he cooked her a delicious meal, accompanied by a good French wine. She was being wooed and she appreciated it. After dinner he invited her to take a shower while he prepared the bedroom. When she entered the room wrapped in a towel she was surprised to see there were candles everywhere, casting a warm glow. Bill was wearing tight leather trousers and an open silk shirt. He presented her with some beautiful lingerie and a pair of soft black, thigh-high, fully zipped leather boots in her size and asked if she would wear them for him. So far, so good . . .

Then he showed her a pair of hand-cuffs and a silk blindfold. Mary was intrigued – this was very different from their usual sexual encounters.

'What are you going to do to me?' she asked tentatively.

'Nothing that you don't agree to,' he replied, pulling on a pair of leather gloves.

'Will you spank me?'

'Only if you want me to.'

'Then what?'

'Oh, I'm sure I can think of something,' he said, smiling at her.

Despite her apprehension she still felt intrigued.

Bill pointed to the bedside table where she could just about make out in the darkness a few different-shaped sex toys in various sizes: vibrators, dildos, a couple of bulldog clips (what could they be for?) and some other items she wasn't familiar with. She also noticed a black leather whip. Oh my God, was she ready for this? How far could she go? He kissed her and she felt the sensuous textures of silk and leather on her skin.

As they lay back on the bed she said, 'You want me to be your sex slave, don't you?' He kissed her breast and moved a gloved hand up her thigh. Suddenly she sat up and looked him in the eye.

'First, you have to be mine. I don't know if I can trust you, so you have to prove it to me,' she told him.

In one go, Mary had switched the power. Bill was amazed but very, very pleased. She was beginning to enjoy this. He did not resist as she undressed him, put the cuffs and blindfold on him and started telling him in no uncertain terms what she was going to do to him. He laughed and said, 'We need a safe word for you to stop, but I'm sure I won't need it.'

'No talking!' she said and she slapped him lightly on the thigh. 'Turn over, now!'

He obeyed and she smacked him hard.

That was just the start of it. At first she was hesitant, but when he encouraged her verbally, she told him to shut up – she was in charge. She spent a good hour exploring his body every which way with various different moves and toys, inflicting more and more pain on him, but he never used the safe word. This was all a bit weird and Mary felt slightly guilty and ashamed, but she was in complete control, which was exhilarating and a real turn-on. She felt she could trust him because he obviously trusted her. When she finally allowed him to penetrate her, she was more aroused than she had ever been.

They slept for a while and then it was his turn; they swapped roles. By now her fantasies were coming thick and fast and she was ready to totally yield and submit to him as he had to her. She was quite scared but she went with it partly out of curiosity to see just how far she could go and how far he would test her. It was touch and go but she allowed herself to go with the pain.

This journey of sexual exploration and experimentation lasted all weekend. It was the most intense sex

Mary had ever had, but it made her feel depersonalised, unreal too. There was mutual trust, but the intimacy felt clinical despite how much they had dared to share with each other. There was no way she could maintain that heightened level of arousal; she would burn out.

Afterwards the pair had a long discussion and agreed to save the BDSM for holidays and special occasions. They had never talked so frankly about their sexuality, and that made Mary feel closer to Bill. Following this episode she came to see me on her own because she wanted my professional opinion.

'Am I normal? Is it OK to do this?' she asked.

'Yes,' I said, 'as long as there is mutual consent and a codeword for "Stop". Be open with each other and keep talking.'

That was all she needed to hear. Sometimes one-session therapy is all it takes.

***

BDSM (Bondage and Domination, Sadism and Masochism) seems to have become almost mainstream in current sexual behaviour, along with the use of a variety of sex toys and dressing-up costumes. Could there be a connection with changing gender roles? Do powerful women need chastising? Often they want their lovers to be stronger than they are, and yet many men willingly submit to the sexual administrations of a dominatrix. Are we becoming desensitised and driven to explore the wilder shores of sexuality? Do we really need pain in order to experience pleasure? Acting out our fantasies can be dangerously exciting.

'Vanilla' sex is straightforward, ordinary and uncomplicated sex that is widely practised and satisfies many of us. It is named after a sweet-smelling spice with a sensual taste and the world's favourite ice cream. Sex can be different every time without necessarily resorting to dressing up or sado-masochistic practices.

Sometimes our sexuality can be distorted or disturbed, usually because of specific messages and experiences from our childhood. An example of this can be found in BDSM practices when taken to an extreme. Sex play is one thing, but a specific ritualistic compulsion is quite another. Tracey's story below is a good illustration of this.

Beat me!

'When I was a little girl and my dad wanted to punish me, he'd make me kneel on all fours on the bed, with my pants pulled down. He'd stand behind me and whack my naked bum with his hairbrush. He'd grunt and I'd scream. I was terrified the first few times but I learnt to put up with it. Then in a weird way I almost looked forward to it – there was a subtle pleasure behind the pain. That's how I like to have sex now – my partner makes me beg for it while he beats me. I tell him how bad I have been. He shouts insults at me and then I have to tell him how wonderful and strong he is as he takes me from behind. A lot of the time it's anal sex or both but he never tells me before he does it. The pain turns me on. My sex life is my dirty secret – I feel ashamed and humiliated, but I also get very aroused . . .'

Tracey obviously found it very difficult to talk about her sexuality. Did she want to change? I wasn't sure. We looked at the good things in her relationship; she did not want to lose her partner. Could he modify his behaviour? It came down to power. How could she claim some power? It would mean learning to be more assertive, to say 'no' and be taken seriously. She also needed to state what was non-negotiable and what could be negotiated. This meant setting some firm boundaries and risking her partner's displeasure.

It was a big change for Tracey. The hardest part for her, though, was coming to terms with her past and the authoritarian, punishing father who also took pleasure in beating her. While she was in therapy, she told her partner she would not have sex with him for the time being. Surprisingly, he accepted this. After eight months she felt ready to rebuild their sexual relationship from scratch. 'Let's try some sex therapy exercises,' I suggested when they came to see me. She was keen and her partner seemed relieved. I explained the programme to them as described in the final chapter of this book, page 169. Eventually the domination side of their lovemaking became lighter, playful even, and they learned to enjoy themselves in simpler ways as well.

Silk knickers

'I wear my wife's knickers because they are soft and silky and they turn me on . . .'

Terry was a cross-dresser and his wife Julie was fed up with it. She did not mind dressing up in soft creamy lingerie and stockings for him but she hated seeing her husband in women's clothing, full make-up and a wig.

The youngest of four, Terry was the only boy and his mother's favourite. His father had abandoned the family soon after his birth. Terry's mother kept him in her bed until he went to primary school. She walked about the house in her underwear and wore silk nighties and soft underwear, always in pastel colours. She would ask him to help her dress and undress. He remembers crawling around on the floor and looking up at her soft white thighs, half hidden by her silky pink slip. At night in bed he would snuggle up to her and revel in her sensual warmth and the slippery texture of her nightie. He liked to hold his penis while he was touching her.

In adolescence, Terry took a pair of his mother's knickers out of her chest of drawers and used them for masturbation. Eventually he started wearing them when he masturbated. Soon he was wearing them all the time.

Terry knew Julie from school. They started dating when they were sixteen and were soon having sex together. Julie was really surprised when Terry bought her nice lingerie and she did not mind wearing it for sex.

Even when he started wearing it 'for fun' she went along with it. The pair married when they were nineteen.

They worked in a local hairdresser's. Terry inherited some money from his grandfather and bought into the business. Eventually he became a partner and Julie was the salon manager. Terry's office opened up onto the salon – 'I just love working there, next to the hum of the dryers, the swish of the pale silky wraps, the smell of shampoo, the sound of women's voices . . . I love women,' he told me. It reminded him of being around his mother as she bathed or washed her hair. Often he had an erection as he walked up and down the salon.

Terry started wearing women's clothing at home after their two children had gone to bed. Dressing as a woman both thrilled and soothed him. Under the skirt inside the silk knickers was his secret weapon, his erect penis. He wanted to cross-dress at work, but he knew Julie would not allow it. However, he had found a pub with a very mixed clientele where he could be Tessie, his alter ego. Cross-dressing gave him an extrovert flashy persona in which he revelled.

Julie was ashamed. While she had protected the children from Terry's habit, she feared he was getting bolder. She did not want him to go out in public dressed as a woman and certainly not with her (she knew Terry was fantasising about it because he had told her).

Julie came from a family of passive, compliant women who did as they were told, but she was determined not to be a doormat like her mother. She was attracted to

Terry because of his feminine side. He would not tell her what to do, but this was the way he exercised his power over her. Julie was realistic: the business was going well, money problems had eased and Terry was a caring father. Sex was literally a bit of a performance, but they loved each other.

And so they came to a compromise: 'I made Terry promise never to go out in public with me as Tessie, or cross-dress in front of the children, but I know he'll never stop doing it,' she told me.

Julie was right: cross-dressers do not wish to give up their habit because they get great satisfaction and a perverse power from it. The status quo suits them so they see no gain in changing. Partners, if they wish to stay together, need to find a way of understanding and living with it.

Blue velvet

Wherever he went, Dave carried a scrap of blue velvet in his front trouser pocket. Often he would put his hand in his pocket to touch it with a mix of guilt and pleasure. Sometimes he would wear Y-fronts instead of boxer shorts so that he could tuck the piece in next to his genitals. He would feel it as he was walking along and it would usually give him an erection. It was both thrilling and comforting.

Dave did a lot of Internet dating, but, to start with, he never mentioned his love of velvet. He was meeting a young woman that evening. It was their fifth date and he was getting all the right signals from her. She seemed a very giving person, who would be understanding – anyway, it was nothing to be ashamed of.

The evening went well and they ended up going back to his place. When he opened the front door, the flat was dark. He took her into the living room and turned on a couple of low lights. While Dave was fixing some drinks in the kitchen she looked round the room in amazement. The curtains were heavy red velvet and the sofa was upholstered in blue velvet and covered in velvet cushions in all colours: pink, purple, turquoise, yellow and green. What was going on here? It was a cross between an Edwardian brothel and hippy heaven (the latter, she hoped). She found the bedroom and took a quick look inside – it was the same scenario, velvet everywhere.

By the time they got to the bedroom she was quite excited. They started undressing. He brought out two velvet bathrobes from the bathroom, one red and one blue. 'Would you put this on?' he asked tentatively. Why not? she thought. It was harmless enough. She wrapped it round her and tied the belt about her waist. They lay down in their velvet robes on top of the velvet bedspread, with velvet cushions under their heads. She felt a little suffocated, but what the hell! Sexually, he was very gentle with her. He enjoyed the cuddling more than the act itself and his erection was not very hard but she didn't mind.

Dave's mother was a sixties hippy who wore flowers in her hair, face-paint, purple nail varnish, sandals, long, brightly coloured Indian scarves and beads and velvet skirts, waistcoats, trousers and jackets. She ran a fashionable boutique, where she sold all the things she liked and had picked up on her trips to India. A lot of the clothes she made herself in a big studio at the back of the shop. Dave was always with her when he was a baby, dressed in little velvet trousers over his nappy; often snuggled up against her breasts, feeding whenever he wanted. He would play on the floor with the pieces of velvet that she cut from the cloth before sewing them up on her ancient machine or stitching and embroidering them by hand. If she ran out of nappies he would roll around naked on the floor in piles of discarded velvet, laughing and burbling. He loved the softness against his skin.

Dave slept in his mother's bed for the first six years because she found it comforting. Apart from the occasional stoned lover she had no one else to share it with. She would sleep naked but she had a blue velvet robe on the bed. Dave would wriggle and snuggle up in it, one hand on his penis and the other on her breast. And when he sucked his thumb he held a scrap of velvet to his cheek or genitals. Bliss! He would drift away in a sensual, happy haze.

'I never did find out who my father was. I'm not sure she knew either. Anyway, we didn't need him, did we? You don't miss what you don't know,' he told me in one of our sessions. He was quite unaware that his relationship with his mother had been quasi-incestuous.

As Dave grew older he made sure to always have a piece of velvet somewhere on his person – it was his secret talisman. He soon found out in bed that rubbing his penis with it made it hard, and before long he was masturbating with velvet, often in his mother's robe or against a cushion. Later she didn't mind him bringing girls home and they would cuddle up with him. By now he had his own bed at the back of her studio, with velvet garments and cushions and cuttings everywhere. The girls found it cool, so bohemian. They weren't aware that he needed the velvet in order to get any kind of an erection and that he only ever had an orgasm if he was touching or holding something velvet. He wasn't even sure he really liked sex.

Dave's mother died of hepatitis when he was forty-two. He kept all her velvet stuff. Most of his girl-friends didn't understand that he had been conditioned from a very young age to respond to certain stimuli. Velvet was his fetish and he wasn't about to give it up; he couldn't. His fragile sexuality was literally too wrapped up in it.

It's almost impossible for fetishists to give up their object of desire, just as cross-dressers will not usually give up their habit. 'I'm OK with that,' Dave told me, 'I don't really want the sex, I want the comfort of holding someone in velvet.'

Insights from the therapist

Both Terry and Dave were fatherless by the time they were three years old. According to Freud's theory of sexual development, this is the Oedipal phase, the age when little boys want to symbolically 'kill' their fathers and 'marry' their mothers.

It's at this time that the child is aware at some unconscious level that his parents are in a sexual relationship; also a time when a little boy is very much in love with his mother but he no longer has sole claim to her. Though jealous of his father (whom he perceives as a rival), he needs to identify with him as a gender role model. The child may desire his mother and fear his father but he cannot have an erotic relationship with his mother. He wants to challenge his father but he must overcome his incestuous love for his mother without feeling guilty towards either of them. Little boys often say 'I want to marry you, Mummy' or 'Go away, Daddy, I hate you!'

But Daddy sometimes does go away and both Terry and Dave won the Oedipal battle for Mummy. Their adult sexual stimuli were formed at this time, creating Terry's fetish for his mother's clothing, which led to his cross-dressing and Dave's fetish for the velvet that surrounded his mother. Neither mother set strong boundaries when their boys were small and their relationships with their sons were not a little incestuous. As adults, both men were ambiguous about sex because their conscious adult desire was at odds with their unconscious incest taboo and their fear of forbidden sex.

Daughters also fall in love with their fathers, but little girls do not have to separate from their mothers in order to find their gender identity. The fantasy erotic relationship is with the father and the incest taboo applies here too, but they do not have to give up any unfulfilled wish about the mother, merely to come to terms with her as a role model. This is one explanation for the rarity of fetishism in women.

CHAPTER SEVEN

Senior Sex

Sexy at sixty

Rachel's husband Stephen had died very suddenly of a heart attack when they were both fifty-five. There had been no warning and she was shocked and distraught. They had been together for over thirty years and on the whole it had been a good marriage. He was a GP in a busy rural practice and she was an occupational therapist. They had brought up two boys, who were both through university. The younger one, Dan, was still living at home.

Their sex life had been very passionate before the children were born but they had realistic expectations of each other and had settled down into a routine afterwards. It was harder to find time alone together as their careers became more demanding and the children grew older, although Rachel chose to work part-time. They made a point of going away alone together for a weekend a few times a year, which was fun. Most of the time their sexual encounters occurred rather perfunctorily when they went to bed at night. Usually they were too exhausted, so it did not happen that often, every few weeks or so. When they did make love, they both knew the moves; they got mutual satisfaction but it was efficient without being exciting. However, it kept them close and they loved each other.

After Stephen's death the last thing on Rachel's mind was sex. She was deeply bereaved and it took her a good two years to get through the loss and mourning. Life carried on, her friends and family were supportive and understanding; she still enjoyed her work. She did not feel lonely, she felt solitary. Rachel got a dog – Stephen had always been a cat man and had not liked dogs. She joined a reading group in the village, and a hiking club, which organised long walks once a month.

When Rachel turned sixty she had a party and tried to celebrate the start of a new decade, her seventieth. It felt quite scary – she was closer to the end of her life than she had realised, yet, with luck, she had another thirty years.

'Will I ever have sex again?' she asked herself. 'Can I really be celibate for the rest of my life?'

When she next undressed she looked at herself naked in the mirror. A bit saggy and flabby, slightly overweight but all right, still curvy, she thought. That night she used her vibrator and fantasised about meeting a man.

Rachel started looking at dating sites, feeling her way around the coded language. She told no one, it was her private secret – she didn't want to be judged. After half a dozen fruitless encounters with various liars and losers she put it out of her mind and resigned herself to a life of celibacy.

A few months later she went on a hike with her club, where she met Jim. There was good chemistry between them, although he wasn't really her type. Jim worked in IT, was divorced and lived on the other side of the county from her, an hour and a half's drive away.

He courted her slowly and carefully, like an old-fashioned gentleman. It was quite exciting. She found herself buying attractive underwear and paying more attention to her personal grooming. There was nothing to lose, she felt. When the time felt right she went back with him to his home and they had sex. They were both very nervous and it wasn't brilliant at first.

'I felt like a virgin again, I didn't know what to expect – his way of touching me and his movements were so different from what I had known. I felt very relieved afterwards. Of course I made him wear a condom, I didn't know what he'd been up to,' she told me.

They soon got into the swing of it and Rachel was surprised at how good it felt. With Jim she felt liberated – they had no shared history, no arguments, no resentments, no shared family. She did not want to live with him (she had become quite set in her ways on her own, a little selfish even). Besides, she had no intention of leaving her home or her village, not to mention Dan and the dog. Seeing Jim every ten days or so with the occasional weekend suited her fine. After all, she had married the love of her life – this was a nice postscript.

She felt confident enough to tell him what she wanted sexually and to give him what he liked. They tried things neither of them had ever done before, which was fun. Their age and experience meant that they had few inhibitions left. There was no such word as failure in their sexual relationship; they were both grateful to have found each other at this stage in their lives.

***

Hugh and Celia came to see me because they were divorcing. Both in their late-fifties, they were looking sleek. Celia was a handsome, intelligent woman who had been married for thirty years, brought up two children and managed a successful career running her own interior design company. Her husband Hugh was a hard-working corporate lawyer who had made a lot of money but was not growing old gracefully. He had fallen for a much younger colleague and for some time had been having a secret affair. She was putting pressure on him to leave his wife. Certainly his marriage had become pretty stale, but then again he had not expected much else at this stage. Now he was thinking that he had probably lived more than half his allotted time-span and that he should make the most of what was left: a fresh start was just what he needed to hold onto youthfulness. Celia didn't seem to need him, the kids had gone – a new relationship would be good for him.

Celia had always known that Hugh was a selfish man, but she was very angry that he could end their marriage in such a way. 'I have always known Hugh was very selfish,' she told me, 'but I'm really hacked off that he has left me for a younger woman.' For professional reasons Hugh wanted to regularise the situation as quickly as possible. Celia was doing her best not to feel bitter, and although she agreed to a quickie divorce, she made him pay for it – 'I got a very good settlement because he felt guilty, I suppose. He can certainly afford it.' She had sold the family home and bought herself the perfect house, which she redesigned according to her own taste.

Soon I was seeing them separately. Hugh was thrilled with his new relationship, telling me, 'I adore my wife and I've got a whole new lease of life.' Sex was exciting again, and he felt invigorated. But once the honeymoon period was over and they settled down into a routine, he started having erectile problems. She wanted to make love every night and some mornings as well. He thought that twice a week was pretty good going. She asked him to take Viagra. He consulted his GP, who ran some tests and gave him a prescription for Cialis, a more up-to-date version that takes effect more rapidly. These drugs work by controlling one enzyme that acts on a second enzyme, which in turn expands the veins in the penis, thereby enabling an erection. However, they do not work unless there is desire and a signal from the brain to release the first enzyme.

Meanwhile, Celia had met a younger man at a party held by one of her clients – much younger, only just in his thirties. He was attracted to her maturity and wisdom and had found women of his own age demanding and critical. Here was someone who appreciated him and supported him. The sex was wonderful too – she knew what she wanted and was not shy about asking for it.

Celia was in heaven. She had overcome her vaginal dryness with the adept use of a good lubricant, and at first she asked him to use a condom because she did not know his past history. Her confidence attracted him and she felt liberated and fulfilled. She did not know how long this relationship would last, but there was no doubt that he had fallen in love with her. To have experienced this now at this stage in her life was a blessing and she would make the most of it.

This couple had turned what could have been a nasty divorce into something positive on both sides. They knew that nothing was perfect, yet each had found some fulfilment and pleasure at an age when many divorced people find themselves alone. Was it luck or sheer determination?

Midlife and ageing

Midlife can be a challenging time. You may find yourself coping with stroppy teenagers, ageing parents, the menopause and existential angst about the meaning of life. Add in stresses at work and concerns about money and there will not be much time or energy left for sex. Do you both still want to have a sex life? This may be a flashpoint for your sexual relationship. If it's not properly nurtured, it could simply curl up and die.

Midlife is when we begin to realise that half our life is over and there are ambitions and fantasies that will probably never be fulfilled. We are aware that we are no longer immortal. This may make us feel anxious and confused, or lonely and depressed. On the positive side, this is also a time of productivity and stability, a chance to consolidate one's successes, to reap the rewards, both personally and professionally, and to explore new activities perhaps more appropriate than Harley-Davidsons and sky-diving.

We may be in our prime at a younger age, but like Rachel and Celia, we still have the chance to reach our sexual potential in midlife. On the whole we are more experienced, more mature and more confident. We are also more realistic and more accepting.

Women's experience of midlife is grounded in the physical reality of the menopause, which can take as long as five years, and usually occurs between the ages of forty-five and fifty-five. For some women the hormonal swings, hot flushes and changing moods signal the end of desire. This may also be true of some men with fluctuating testosterone levels and erection problems. Some couples may no longer be interested in pursuing a sexual relationship, which is fine if they both feel the same way about no longer having sex.

The menopause confirms that a woman's fertility is over. With it come various aspects of physical decline and the fear of loss of status in the outside world. However, the post-war generation, with increasing wellbeing, longevity and standard of living, are the pioneers of a new model: active, independent, strong, sexual women who are successfully running families, households and careers. If their partners can share their renewed energy and interests the relationship can move on through the midlife period with increased stability and enjoyment.

Sadly, midlife can often be a time of separation and divorce, which is what happened with Hugh and Celia. This means coming to terms with loss and feelings of failure just when one is moving on towards old age and need to feel secure and stable. The majority of men who find themselves on their own in midlife will look for another partner rather than face growing old alone. There is no doubt that at this stage in life age favours men in terms of attractiveness and eligibility. From an evolutionary point of view middle-aged men will seek out women who are still fertile. These younger women are unconsciously drawn to older men as providers and protectors.

As for women alone in midlife, nature is not fair. As they go through the hormonal ups and downs of the menopause, which affects their looks as well as their moods, many of them find themselves alone, whether or not they choose to be. The evolutionary purpose of post-menopausal women is to help their daughters raise grandchildren. Of course this does not always fit in with the society in which we live. Many women feel a renewed sense of liberation and energy after the menopause and continue to lead independent, busy and rewarding lives. What about sex? Some feel relieved their sex life is over; others feel relieved that the menopause is over but their sexuality lives on. An increasing number like Celia are turning towards younger men.

Insights from the therapist

'I'm a Type 2 diabetic, which means I have problems with my erections, but it doesn't stop us from having quite sexy cuddles. I can give and receive pleasure in other ways...'

In old age many of us will be affected by illness, chronic health conditions and surgery as well as treatments such as chemotherapy and radiotherapy. The more common ones that can affect sexual activity include arthritis, osteoporosis, diabetes, cancer and neurological diseases. Medication for any of these conditions may have unwanted side-effects which affect sexual desire and performance.

We need to acknowledge our limitations and work with these conditions. It may be hard accepting the changes to our bodies, the brutal reality of old age, especially if we have undergone major surgical procedures such as mastectomy or prostatectomy, which are closely connected to our sexuality. We need to chase away feelings of fear, anxiety and shame and hold onto self-esteem despite our changed body image. Given the right encouragement, we can still discover a different kind of good sex. For example: 'I had to have a double mastectomy, which was absolutely devastating. I couldn't be naked or look at myself in the mirror for months. I felt ashamed of my ruined body; I would sleep all scrunched up. Night after night I cried and mourned my lost breasts. Any sexual contact was out of the question. Finally my partner got fed up with me and we had a massive row. He told me I was one of the lucky ones because I was still alive and well. We had a hug and slept in each other's arms that night.'

This is where physical contact with a caring and supportive partner can be a source of great comfort. Touch and affection, hand-holding and strokes, kisses and hugs will keep isolation and loneliness at bay. Unfortunately hospitals, retirement homes and care homes are still insufficiently enlightened to understand and accept that sexual contact between old people is not only acceptable but can be positively healing. Many suffer from undiagnosed depression, which can be a terrible burden at this late stage of their lives. We need to pay attention to each other as carers.

This is a time when we will inevitably be dealing with the loss of relatives and friends as well as our own loss of youth. As we face our own death we must find detachment and peace of mind. The sexual drive can be present in some people until the day they die; their sexuality may still be experienced in old age as a vital part of who they are. Good sex helps one feel alive and improves the quality of life.

Get it while you can, enjoy the moment – this is a precious time.

CHAPTER EIGHT

Gender Wars

Who does what?

David and Jenny were in their early thirties. David ran his own business from home, while Jenny was a successful solicitor. Both were achievers with high expectations. Jenny worked hard and was professionally ambitious. A strong, modern, independent young woman, she demanded a lot of herself and of David. She had a younger sister with whom she had been in competition throughout her life for their father's love and attention. Also a solicitor, her father was proud that she had chosen the same career as him and that she was so successful. Her mother, who was a quiet, browbeaten woman, had never worked and did not understand her at all. Jenny did not want to be like her mother.

David ran a landscape gardening business, which was affected by the economic climate, and he was currently earning less than Jenny. They shared all the household chores. Their sex life had dwindled to nothing. David felt rejected and unloved. Jenny was just too busy, too stressed and too tired.

The youngest of four, David was close to his mother but he had seen what hard work it was for her to run the house and raise the family with no help from her husband. His father was away a lot on business and his relationship with his children was somewhat cool and distant. David was determined not to repeat the traditional pattern of his parents' marriage. Part of his attraction to Jenny was that she was so unlike his mother, but she seemed to have lost her energy and enthusiasm and, like his mother, complained of being tired all the time.

'We will probably have to take on a nanny or an au pair to help with the childcare,' he told Jenny. She liked that idea.

Jenny had been attracted to David's entrepreneurial spirit. She was ambitious, like her father, and she had not realised how laid-back David was. Luckily she was earning a very good salary. She wanted children, but not yet.

In therapy we explored their gender expectations. Consciously, they were meeting each other's needs for equality; unconsciously, things were very different.

'I have always admired Jenny's professional success but I have felt rather emasculated. I am fed up with working at home,' said David.

Jenny was of the view: 'I wanted David and me to be completely equal. My dad did nothing in the home and my mum was a doormat and I didn't want to end up like her.'

They agreed that sacrifices had to be made in order to improve their relationship. Jenny managed to change her role at work and work shorter hours and agreed to try for a baby. David took the risk of diversifying and moving his business to outside premises. They also made time for each other.

Through our sessions Jenny realised that she had idealised her father and that David was not a replica of him. David knew that when they had a baby, Jenny would never be a doormat like her mother and he would never be a distant father like his father.

Jenny had always been sexually confident and assertive. She realised that secretly she wanted her partner to be sexually more dominant than her. David had been holding back but was reassured when Jenny told him she wanted him to be more assertive in bed. Desire was reignited and both were thrilled to have a satisfying sex life again.

> 'I had no idea! I didn't want to come across as a caveman but I am thrilled to be more macho in bed.'

> 'I am definitely attracted to him again now that he has become proactive and can take the initiative.'

These changes took a while. Eventually they adjusted to their new roles and were able to renew their sexual relationship in the hope of Jenny getting pregnant. They found new attraction and admiration in each other.

Both felt optimistic and more empowered. They were relieved to have found a way of giving their lives as a couple more meaning and the sex really improved once they got going again.

Many men unconsciously want their partners to care and look after them as well as their mothers did (or should have). And many women still want men to be in charge and take responsibility so that they can spend more time with their babies and small children. Both men and women want a better quality of life. This may have to be negotiated with honesty in relation to each partner's true feelings and not with a politically correct vision of how it all ought to be. Some couples living together with equal gender roles can end up like flatmates or siblings. There is no gender differentiation, they are both neutralised – they have lost touch with their instinctual drive for sex.

Who's in charge?

'We never have sex anymore – I'm fed up! We have rows instead.'

'You bully me all the time, of course I'm angry.'

'We have stupid arguments about the washing-up!'

'I do most of the chores around here, it's the least you could do!'

This was a familiar pattern with Sam and Ellen.

Sam was Italian, charming, social; extrovert. Ellen was Scottish, cool, mysterious; more reticent. They were opposites, which made their relationship hard work. He was forty-one, she was thirty-nine; they had been together for fourteen years and had a twelve-year-old son. Sam would have liked at least one more child, but Ellen's experience of pregnancy and childbirth had been very negative and she refused to consider it.

The youngest of four children, Sam's parents divorced when he was six. His mother had several lovers after the divorce. She was dominating and possessive but much admired by him. He did not see his father again until he was eighteen.

Ellen was the second of four children. Her parents had always put their marriage first, the children second. Her father was controlling, aggressive and intimidating. Her mother always prioritised her husband's needs and was very submissive. Ellen had felt neglected.

Sam and Ellen had met and lived together in New York. It had been a carefree, romantic time and they decided they wanted a baby.

When Ellen was seven months pregnant they married and moved to Milan. She did not enjoy being pregnant. Sam was extremely unsupportive after the birth – 'I felt displaced and for the first few months I admit I didn't really connect with the baby,' he explained. 'Ellen gave him all her attention and I'm ashamed to say I was quite jealous. My father died around that time and I needed her support.'

'It seems neither of you was able to support the other, you both felt neglected,' I observed.

'Yes, I felt very isolated,' said Ellen, 'and quite depressed too. I didn't speak Italian so I couldn't work in Milan and I did not get on with my mother-in-law, who was always interfering.'

By the time Sam and Ellen moved to London, two years later, they were already arguing the whole time. Sam was the one who always wanted sex but Ellen kept turning him down. He felt rejected, she felt criticised. When he attacked her verbally, she withdrew even more sexually. They were not able to function as a couple, or understand how the other was feeling. Sam would bully Ellen and boss her about in a controlling and authoritative way. She reacted as she did to her father, with fear and distrust, but she gave as good as she got and they would end up shouting at each other.

Sam said he was afraid that Ellen might be unfaithful, which is how his mother had behaved. Sex would have reassured him. Ellen in turn revealed that she had a fear of becoming a submissive wife like her mother. Also, she had fears about her own competence as a wife and mother – she wasn't very good at being domestic. She wasn't even thinking about sex or missing it.

Sam was worried that if Ellen became too independent he would end up leaving her before she left him, just as his father had left his mother. As far as he was concerned, feeling rejected and unloved and not having sex would be reason enough to leave her. Sam came to realise that he actually wanted a traditional wife who would run the house and be loving and giving, someone who would admire him. He had imagined Ellen could fulfil that role but she was very ambivalent about the traditional role of wife and mother. She wanted a more equal relationship with more sharing of domestic responsibilities and greater independence. Meanwhile she had become defensive and unable to give Sam any affection, let alone sex.

Neither Sam nor Ellen had been given much physical affection in childhood and they had very different expectations of marriage and parenthood. Their romantic fantasy was fading fast. Lack of parental attention had made him needy and demanding but had made her punishing and withholding. This was reflected in their sexual relationship. They were confused about what they had wished for and how things really were. It turned out they did not really know or understand each other at all; they had idealised each other and the reality was very different. Sam had thought Ellen came from a traditional and united family and she could replicate that for him. She had thought he would be the opposite of her tyrannical father. In reality neither could give the other what he or she wanted or expected, and this was played out in their sexual power struggle and constant arguing. Sam admitted how powerful his mother was and that he really did not want Ellen to be like her. He also understood that his controlling, aggressive behaviour scared Ellen because it reminded her of her father.

When Sam said he was ready to let go of his unrealistically high expectations of the relationship, Ellen became even more controlling and emasculating. Was it too late for her? He was weak, as well as a bully. She was winning the power struggle but losing the marriage. Sam was talking about separation and had gone as far as finding somewhere else to live. Was it over? He could walk away wounded and hurt, blaming the lack of sex. After all, women were bitches. She could be bitter and tell herself that all he really wanted from her was more sex. Men were so cruel.

In the end they both realised they had to accept the other as they really were and let go of anger from the past. Fortunately they both felt it was better to work on their marriage than to let it go, and so we ended the therapy on a hopeful note.

Insights from the therapist

The biggest question for the post-feminist modern woman is can she have it all? Can she successfully juggle her career, marriage and the home without making sacrifices? Can she be Superwoman? Women are now as well educated as men, if not better, and have choices about planning babies. But they cannot be full-time mothers without stepping off the career ladder. Even part-time mothers lose out professionally and often feel guilty about not fulfilling either role satisfactorily.

The stereotypical view of women is that they are nurturing, maternal, caring, emotionally expressive and responsive, empathic and communicative, patient and resourceful multi-taskers, sexually passive and submissive. High-flying Alpha women are strong and confident, ambitious and high achievers and often out-earning their partners. They are clever, competent and successful, with high expectations of themselves and others. But are they too bossy and demanding and with men who often complain that women have a checklist they can't live up to? Are they perceived as emasculating?

The male stereotype is that the man is the provider and protector. He is strong, reliable and confident, driven by ambition and success. Men are assertive and competitive, solution-oriented and problem solving. Analytical, logical and rational thinkers, they set themselves tasks and objectives and don't talk about their feelings. They may be emotionally repressed and poor communicators, but they have a high sex drive; they can also get angry and violent.

Men are no longer valued for their traditional masculine qualities. Some earn less than their partners, or, worse still, are redundant and unemployed. They used to be tribal hunter-gatherers but now they are deprived of the chase and watch football instead.

'I'm just a bloke, let me be blokeish!' they cry.

Education has been increasingly feminised, with the emphasis on co-operation, not competition, the group, not the individual. This has not necessarily been helpful to boys. New man is often disillusioned and disempowered, he may feel insecure and inadequate. He is accused of being immature and weak, mocked and put down. Little wonder he feels bewildered.

Metrosexual man is into grooming and waxing products, wearing Lycra-control underwear, even having plastic surgery because of poor body image. Sensitive and nurturing, he is happy to share child rearing and be an attentive house husband. He may be intuitive and creative, but is he happy? Do Alpha females want to be with Beta males, or do they actually wish for an Alpha male? Two Alphas can often lead to competitive conflict.

Can it be true that men are from Mars, women are from Venus?

'Men need sex in order to feel intimate, women want intimacy in order to feel sexy.'

'For some women sex is the price they pay to be in a relationship. Some men stay in a relationship in order to have regular sex.'

'Women want romance, men want variety; women are looking for commitment, men just want pleasure.'

'Men can boast about their sexual conquests, women who boast about theirs are sluts.'

Obviously these generalisations are very black and white and it's important to challenge them. But where does that leave sex? Are men being emasculated by strong, pushy women? Is this women's revenge against centuries of patriarchal power, and is this why there is so much interest in bondage and domination? In sexual role play women can be submissive to commanding men, or men may be punished by a dominatrix.

Gender roles are being blurred. When men and women move away from their gender identity in the name of equality there is a danger of being neutered and then desire fades. Couples end up living in sexless relationships like siblings or flatmates. We need to feel differentiated.

Men and women can be equal but different; their sexuality lies in this difference. The sexes share forty-five chromosomes. In the forty-sixth women are XX, men XY. That Y chromosome makes all the difference – we need to value this difference without giving up the idea of equality.

The reproductive sex act involves the man putting his erect penis into her receptive vagina; the sperm then has to enter the egg. She can be passive, he needs to be active – these are the basic facts of life. Our sexuality and our sexual identity are found in both our sex and our gender. Gender may be influenced by our social, cultural and psychological environment but sex is biological. Currently, gender seems to be more fluid, more on a spectrum, but your sex is undeniable – you are born male or female (with very rare exceptions).

What will happen to sex if men become more marginalised and women escape their biological destiny? Is there some slow evolutionary process at work, some kind of natural selection?

The war between the sexes is as old as humankind. Can there be acceptance and reconciliation between men and women; can we respect and celebrate the difference between us?

Let us hope that sex and sexuality can be experienced in the spirit of the sixties slogans 'Peace and love' and 'Make love, not war'.

CHAPTER NINE

Sexual Healing

Let's not do it!

Phil and Anita had been together for five years. Two years into the relationship Anita lost her job and caught a very nasty flu virus, which turned into CFS (Chronic Fatigue Syndrome). This lasted for eighteen months, during which time Phil looked after her with much devotion. Their sexual relationship was fine until Anita fell ill. When she started to feel better and they wanted to resume their sexual activity, Phil developed erection difficulties at the moment of penetration. There was a lot of shared foreplay and mutual masturbation, but Anita wanted full penetrative sex. Phil felt a failure and Anita felt confused.

Phil's mother had breast cancer and was exhausted by her chemotherapy treatment. When he was eighteen, his sister had had a near-fatal car accident and had spent seven months in hospital. Phil had been a good carer – his experience of the women he loved was that they were vulnerable and fragile. And now Anita had joined them.

Anita's parents had divorced when she was ten. Her father had re-married and had two new daughters. Anita felt neglected – he had never made her feel special. She was very close to her mother, who was rather controlling. Phil had helped to give her a lot of confidence, but with her illness, she had lost some of her self-esteem.

'I don't think Phil desires me,' she said in one of our sessions. 'That must be why he keeps losing his erection.'

'I'm sure there must be more to it than that,' I suggested.

'Well, yes,' said Phil. 'I think Anita finds sex painful.'

It transpired that when the couple had resumed their sexual relationship Anita had felt pain on intercourse. She was too embarrassed to talk about this because she felt a failure. Neither of them saw the other as a fully functioning sexual being and so they had both got stuck with this perception; she was an invalid, he was her nurse. He did not want to cause her pain on penetration, whereas she in turn did not want him to feel bad about his loss of erection.

We talked a lot about their concerns and they started a series of sex therapy exercises, as described at the end of this chapter (page 210). This enabled them to become close and intimate again without any pressure to perform, and they gained a lot of insight into their relationship. Eventually Phil stopped worrying about his erection and Anita relaxed. After a while they were able to have penetrative sex without an absolute goal. They both felt much better about themselves and about their relationship.

Bad sex leads to no sex. When sexual problems become unmanageable, sexual activity between couples ceases. Sexual difficulties can have physical causes such as illness, or psychological origins, or a combination of both. The psychological causes may be to do with the relationship or originate in conscious and unconscious messages acquired in childhood. There are myriad reasons for sexual difficulties, often rooted in ignorance and repression, taboos and abuse. These need to be explored before engaging in sex therapy.

Precipitating factors may arise from life events and crises such as illness and trauma, family problems, issues at work, stress and anxiety. This in turn may lead to fear of sexual failure, avoidance and consequent rows and arguments, guilt and shame, lack of communication and fear of intimacy.

The danger of sex

Andrew and Alice wanted to have a baby, but she had suffered a loss of desire since they got married two years previously. They were having sex very occasionally but she felt angry. He had stopped initiating sex because he did not want to be rejected.

Andrew was caring and supportive, and very devoted. He had Alice on a pedestal. Alice was volatile and emotional. She was attracted by Andrew's creativity, which she found quite exciting compared to her dry professional world of accountancy. He in turn found her warm and open, in contrast to his family.

Their sexual relationship was satisfactory at first. They lived together for a year before getting married, which was a joint decision. After they married Alice turned thirty and felt older and less attractive. Sex became perfunctory – she admitted to a fear of commitment. Andrew described their sex life as 'routine, not very adventurous'. Alice said she found it difficult to let go and became more and more restrictive: missionary position only.

Her previous relationships had been short-lived – she had had lots of flings and one-night stands. Sex had been exciting and gratifying but she felt very ambivalent with Andrew. Married sex was not supposed to be raunchy, yet she wanted him to be more assertive.

He understandably felt confused: for him sex was about intimacy and bonding.

Andrew's family were polite and formal – anger was never expressed, sex never discussed. 'I had a holiday fling when I was a student,' he told me during one of our sessions. 'She got pregnant and I have a son whom I have never seen – the girl stopped contacting me.'

He needed to mourn that loss, I thought.

'How did you feel about that?' I asked Alice.

'I was shocked at first,' she admitted, 'but I don't really relate to it – it's in his past. I'm glad he told me, though.'

Alice's family were expressive and argumentative.

She described her father as 'open and creative', but her mother was 'emotional and manipulative' – she was afraid she was like her. Her parents had married because her mother was pregnant. They had split up, got back together, had an unplanned baby who was ten years younger than Alice and had then split up again.

Both Andrew and Alice's experience was that sex led to unwanted pregnancies and trouble. Consciously they wanted a baby, but unconsciously they were afraid.

Alice had no experience of sex with intimacy but felt guilty about enjoying married sex. Professionally ambitious and successful, she was disappointed by Andrew's laid-back attitude to work – and to sex.

Andrew was no longer initiating or responding. I suggested they try a programme of sex therapy exercises, as described further on in this chapter (page 210).

Alice managed to initiate the sex therapy exercises. It went fine at first, but what came out of it was that there were gender issues. She was driven but wanted him to be more macho. He gave her emotional stability but was not allowed to be sexy. She was too dominating; he felt emasculated. Her loss of desire was a way of having control in the relationship, but it was also partly a shared fear and anxiety about commitment.

The exercises helped them find equality and confidence. They were able to communicate about their assumptions and expectations. Once, they broke the rules and had sex, which was her idea. He was thrilled but she got scared and backed off again.

They went back to the beginning and started again but they got to the same point and had a huge row. Both felt hurt and angry and confused. Eventually Andrew took responsibility for all the times he had rejected her – she carried the problem, but now he had to own his part in it. Relieved, Alice started to feel much closer to him.

There were ups and downs throughout the sex therapy, but after many heart-searching talks about their relationship and their fears, Andrew and Alice were able to make love again and were talking about trying for a baby.

This time they meant it.

***

It is quite clear to me from working with people's sexual difficulties that by far the most important sexual organ is the brain, which is far more complex and subtle than the most advanced computer. This is where it all starts.

Most of our sexual problems are of psychological origin, fed by thoughts, feelings, fantasies and the many cultural, social, religious and family messages that we pick up from the moment we are born. Once we understand that we can begin to move beyond these difficulties, we just need to get out of our heads, get physical, keep it simple, relax and enjoy. There is nothing as good as good sex – we owe it to ourselves and to our partners. There can be sexual healing, so let's go for it!

Insights from the therapist

There is a way back to having good sex. First, you must take care of yourself, like yourself, respect yourself and your body. There may be things in your life that you have no control over. Focus on the areas where you can make choices for yourself. Here are some suggestions of how you might do this.

Be in touch with your body; be aware of your moods. When you feel better in your mind and your body, you will feel better about sex.

Aim for some work/life balance to reduce stress and free up time. Try not to work in the evening or at weekends. Take a couple of holidays a year or more, however short, and go for weekends away in between.

Eat a nourishing diet with regular meal times. Never skip breakfast. Drink plenty of water during the day, too.

Find time to exercise, even if it's just walking as you go about your daily life.

Don't overdo alcohol and/or drugs. Stop smoking – help and advice are available from your GP.

Get enough sleep and learn to relax or meditate for ten or fifteen minutes a day.

Spare some time for the activities you enjoy, be they reading, music, cinema, cooking, gardening . . .whatever increases your feelings of wellbeing.

Talk to your partner; share your concerns and your hopes. Listen to theirs and pay attention to each other. Let go of anger; try not to argue and agree to differ. You both need to show willingness and co-operation. Make sure you both have realistic and informed expectations of your sexual relationship.

Try some sex therapy exercises. The following classic exercises were devised by Masters and Johnson, sexologists in the 1960s; they are usually very helpful in one way or another for any sexual difficulty.

Sensate Focus is the most widely used programme in sex therapy and is used to treat all of the major sexual dysfunctions (loss of desire, pain, premature ejaculation, no orgasm, erectile difficulties, vaginal block). It is extremely useful as a diagnostic tool, whether physical, emotional or psychological.

Sensate Focus is a de-sensitisation and gradual exposure programme involving a series of exercises that you agree to do together on a regular basis at home and discuss afterwards. It is a process that removes a major source of anxiety, helps to build trust and improves the level of communication. The exercises may appear to be artificial and lacking in spontaneity. You may feel nervous and embarrassed, resistant and defensive. There needs to be an alliance in your relationship based on mutual trust and respect. Humour can defuse anxiety and bring some fun to the exercises.

The first rule of sex therapy is that you and your partner will agree not to have sexual intercourse for a while. You may say that you are not having intercourse anyway. The difference is that this is an agreed contract between the two of you, a shared commitment. Placing a ban on intercourse removes any pressure to perform – there are no demands or expectations for erections, orgasms or sexual intercourse. It can be very liberating because you can have physical contact without fear of having to perform or deliver and discover what it is like to become close and intimate again in a sensual way.

You need to check for any physical causes for the problem and put the situation in the context of your life-stage. If there has been no sexual intercourse in the relationship for a period of time, you may need to talk about the implications of change before committing to sex therapy. Relationship issues need exploring. You must be motivated enough to make a shared commitment to each other and to the therapy in terms of time and application. Usually the process takes a minimum of three months.

Remind yourselves that there is no goal, no pressure, no expectation, no need to perform; no right or wrong. The emphasis is on getting in touch with the senses, focusing on touch, sight, smell, taste and sound. Sensual, not sexual, it is more about being than doing. Arousal is incidental.

Through these exercises you are given permission to learn what gives you pleasure before giving pleasure to your partner.

The second important rule (after the ban on intercourse) is that each of you will give the other equal time and attention, equal giving and receiving, equal responsibility for setting up the exercises.

At first you are going to learn what gives you pleasure before giving pleasure to your partner.

- Try to carry out this exercise at least once a week.
- Put aside one hour during which you will not be interrupted.
- Choose a private, warm, comfortable place, not necessarily the bedroom. There can be cushions, candles, music, a glass or two of wine, body lotion, oil or talc.
- If you want, you can both take a shower or a bath first, then lie down together naked with some light in the room.
- You are going to take it in turns to touch, stroke and caress each other from top to toe. First, the back of the body, then the front, from head to foot without touching the genitals, buttocks or breasts.
- This exercise is for the giver, not the receiver. It is about rediscovering what it feels like to touch your partner in an intimate and sensual way. It's not about turning your partner on.
- The giver can experiment with different types of touch, experience the different skin textures; explore unfamiliar parts of the body.
- The receiver may ask the giver to stop if he or she experiences anything uncomfortable or unpleasant.

- When the first person has completed the task (twenty to thirty minutes) you change over. It is essential that you each have an equal amount of time.

- If there is any sexual arousal on either side, it can be acknowledged but nothing needs to be done about it. Should either of you experience a desire to masturbate, this can be done alone afterwards.

- Make sure you both fully understand the instructions so that there are no misunderstandings.

- Decide who goes first. The giver is responsible for setting up the date, time and place for the exercise. Take it in turns.

Later on you can de-brief each other.

- What was your overall experience of the exercise?
- How did it feel to be touching?
- How did it feel to be touched?
- What felt good, what felt not so good?
- Were you able to focus?
- What were you thinking?
- Was it easier giving or receiving?
- What did you learn about yourself?
- What did you learn about your partner?

- What were your feelings, sensations and fantasies?

Try to be positive, reassuring and encouraging with each other. You need to deal with relationship issues if you feel any of the following emotions after doing the exercises:

- Anger
- Anxiety
- Guilt
- Shame
- Inhibition
- Fear of intimacy
- Fear of rejection
- Lack of trust
- Power struggle
- Conflict.

Some couples will not trust themselves to lie naked together. They can start by wearing nightwear or underwear and just lie next to each other, holding hands. This may be the most intimacy they can manage at first.

Either partner may be put back in touch with negative experiences of sex, abuse or violence that they may never have talked about. This requires sensitive acknowledgement and understanding.

The exercise is to be repeated on at least three separate occasions or more until you are both completely confident and comfortable with it.

The next exercise is exactly the same as the first, only this time the breasts, buttocks and genitals are included. You may kiss each either and have oral/genital contact as long as it's equal. This is still primarily a sensual exercise with no sexual goal. It is still about the giver exploring the partner's body without any intention of giving pleasure. The receiver may feel pleasure and desire; he may have an erection, she may lubricate. This can be acknowledged, but nothing overtly sexual is done about it.

The exercise enables you to get back in touch with each other's whole body in a sensual, non-demanding way. It also shows you that arousal and desire may occur spontaneously without being strived for.

If either of you is reluctant to do this exercise, go back to the first exercise and start again.

Repeat at least three times or more.

Now you are going to focus on giving each other pleasure, asking the other for what you would each like. Having found out what gives you pleasure, you can now focus on what gives your partner pleasure. Start from the beginning, as before. There is still no goal for orgasm, even though it may occur from mutual stimulation. At this point, however, many couples will break the 'no intercourse' rule and find themselves agreeing to make love. This is fine so long as there is mutual consent and no pressure on either side.

Like the previous exercise, this exercise is repeated until you both feel good about it. Any time there is a block, you need to go back to the first exercise and start again.

The next step is stop/start vaginal containment with the woman sitting astride the man and guiding the tip of his penis in and out of her vagina. There is no movement; this is repeated several times. Again, it is very possible that the ban on intercourse will be broken.

When you are both comfortable with this final exercise you can both start moving. You are now making love – and don't worry about reaching orgasm.

This programme of exercises is extremely effective for most couples because it offers the chance to break old habits, discover what they each really want and rediscover the trust and intimacy they have lost. Sometimes just a temporary ban on intercourse is liberating enough for a couple to get back in touch with each other physically and emotionally, so that they can go from no sex to good sex with a deeper understanding about giving and receiving pleasure.

Resources

Further reading

Godson, Suzi and Agace, Mel, *The Sex Book* (Cassell Illustrated, 2002).

Martin-Sperry, Carol, *Good Sex, Bad Sex, No Sex: A Guide for Grown-Ups* (Endeavour Press Ltd., 2012).

Phillips, Adam, *Monogamy* (Faber & Faber, 1996).

Stephenson-Connolly, Dr Pamela, *Sex Life: How Our Sexual Experiences Define Who We Are* (Vermillion, 2011).

For professional help

British Association for Counselling and Psychotherapy
www.bacp.org

Carol Martin-Sperry
www.shrinkrap.co.uk

College of Sexual and Relationship Therapists
www.cosrt.org

Relate
www.relate.org

Index